This time I'll do it better…

Thinking of Your First Million

in the Stock Market?

Don't Procrastinate…We can do it!

I0462236

JESUS G. PEDINES JR.

TrulyRichClub Member, Entrepreneur, Investor, Author

and OFW Safety Professional.

CONTENTS

Preface

Many individual thinks that Stock Market is too risky and it's only for the rich people. Well, it is true, Stock Market is risky to those active traders especially those newbies. However, Stock Market isn't only for rich people, in fact, everyone can be an investor in the Stock Market. Do you think Stock Market is only for millionaire or billionaire people like Bo Sanchez? Of course not, as I've said, any individual of legal age can invest in the stock market; even your kids.

Now, since you are reading this simple book, you have a chance to know the secret of rich people, you have the opportunity to know and play their games, you have a chance to be like them or be included in the two percent of people who are investing in the stock market. Many Filipino doesn't think that way. Instead, they are thinking the opposite way. Yes! You have a chance because you're doing something.

Think about this. What will happen if you start investing in the Stock Market now? Let's say this month after reading this book? For instance, a few years later and you keep funding account and continuously buying your favorite stocks to grow your portfolio, then you will see many individuals behind you are just starting to do what you did a year ago. Do you get my point? Yes, you will be far away ahead of them, not only the size of your portfolios but in terms of knowledge and skills. That is it. Don't tell yourself you are too late; age doesn't matter, there are many ways to cope up. The train is always there with a million passengers already on their way headings to financial freedom, be one of those people making money in the Stock Market.

Be guided through TrulyRichClub of brother Bo Sanchez. So, why not join the team? Throw all negative thoughts out of the window.

In this book, I will show you how to start by sharing my journey and plans investing in the Philippine Stock Market.

Acknowledgements

Thanks to my family who has been my inspiration in completing this book. To my wife Jingle Lumidao Pedines, to our daughters and our family circle. Indeed, this book would not be a success without your love and support.

To all my Filipino mentors especially to brother Bo Sanchez, Chinkee Tan, and many other international mentors, thank you for guiding me. To all colleagues and friends who trusted my thoughts and advices, thank you.

Above all, thanks and praise to our Almighty Creator for showering us with good health and blessings and for guiding me in the making of this book and more books to come, God willing.

Introduction

First of all, I acknowledged that I am not a professional writer nor financial expert to discuss this subject, but this is not a reason to stop me from writing this book. My primary objective is to share my journey from being an OFW and how I was able to learn about investing in the stock market while working abroad. I hope that you will find beneficial information to guide you based on my personal experience in the world of investing in the Philippine-Stock-Market.

On the year 2009, my wife and I were actively joining MLM business of herbal products and eventually joined a franchise partnership here in Saudi Arabia. During those days, what we know is to give our share hoping to earn some extra income from being a franchise partner. We really don't know what will happen next, we were just hoping that our partners will be managing the business properly. To make the story short, the partnership didn't work out. Fortunately, we were able to get a refund of our capital before the business collapsed. Having said that, maybe we were just lucky, at least we learned a lesson.

On the last quarter of 2012, I was able to attend a financial management presentation rendered by one of my fraternity brother at Riyadh Saudi Arabia. I was amazed and shocked when I came to know about the basic financial management. He talked about the importance of emergency fund, the different kind or types of investment like the stock market, real estate, bonds, etc.

After his presentation, I opened up my mind and gradually developed my desire to learn more. Indeed, he was my first mentor who taught me how to understand the real investing concept and system. Thank you very much, brother Rodel Yap. May we always be in Leadership, Friendship, and Service.

I hope you will find ways to read this book till the last page. If you're considering investing in the Stock Market, this is the break you've been dreaming of, to be a multimillionaire someday. As long as you are willing to understand the basic knowledge about investing, then this is what you're looking for - a basic guide. Though I know that the Internet may provide all information about what I am about to share with you in this book, I still believed that in some way this book has a special approach to help you build that interest to invest in the stock market.

Don't entertain negative thoughts like, "Who is this guy? I can't do this. Why should I trust the advice of this newbies investor? Stock Market is too risky. I don't know how to start. I might lose all my money," and so on and so forth. Well, if you're thinking that way I hope you will be able to reprogram your mindset after reading this book. If you would just spare your time, I will share with you my experience.

Don't be afraid, trust your guts and get rid of those negative thoughts, throw them away, and start learning the game of rich people. In this book, I will show you the ABCs of investing in the Philippine stock market using the approach that I have learned from all my mentors.

This simple book may help you to figure out the know-how to invest in the Philippine Stock Market regardless of your civil status, current job, and achievements just like brother Bo taught his maids to invest in the Stock Market. Is that fair enough? Does that encourage you to acquire financial freedom someday? If not in the Stock Market, you may apply the formula described in this book toward many other investing opportunities you are interested in or to any goals, you may have on your list. My first question is... Do you have the list of your goals? If you already have the list I am talking about, this book may help you boost up your energy on achieving your goals in life. It may turn you to be more energetic going to work every day looking forward to the next 20% of your monthly salary to be invested. Believe me, the key is 'TIME and following the right system.'

As brother Bo Sanchez promised to all TrulyRichClub members, you too will "Gain Financial Wealth" from his system. The earlier we start, the wealthier we become.

Anyway, let's get started. Congratulations for having a copy of this book. I would say you are dedicated to moving forward and learning the know-how to invest in the Stock Market.

However, if you are just curious about it, I promise you'll get something beneficial once you have finished reading this book, whatever your plan is.

A Promise

Yes, you will learn many things in this book; I will share my personal approach and understanding on applying what I have learned from all my mentors. It is all about my personal views and application of what I have learned from them. If you have already read those books that I'll be mentioning, here is my WARNING... you might have different understanding and views on applying the formula. So be it... I don't claim to be a financial adviser as I said, but I believe that sharing my experience and my thoughts would be my simple way to help other people. It doesn't matter if someone will criticize my book, but to me what matters is that I just want to share my experience with you. Yes, you.... Therefore, it is up to you how you process the advices in this book.

Now, if you have had the chance to watch brother Bo Sanchez' videos on YouTube or read his book entitled, "My Maid Invests In The Stock Market And Why You Should Too." You may recall that brother Bo always mentions that "*anyone can be rich or wealthy through Stocks even a domestic helper can invest in the stock market.*" In TrulyRichClub, Brother Bo taught us how to manage our own financial future through the stock market.

Are you willing to start enhancing your financial education? Now if your answer is yes, then I will do all my best to show you at least the tip of the iceberg that may open up your mind as well.

For your information, my idea of making this book is not only for you but for me as well because this book will serve as my trail to attain my new goals in life and I want to share it with you.

As a promise to myself, I will do all my best to take action and accomplish everything necessary to turn all my goals into physical reality. I promise to myself to continue improving my persistence on achieving all my pending goals listed in my diary. I will continuously monitor my strength and weaknesses and be active on searching new opportunities available out there to initiate my plans and to be ready for any threat around me so that I can be able to re-calibrate if needed.

I promise to read more books; as many as I can. I promise to attend, listen, and watch more online trainings and talks related to investing in order to improve my financial literacy. I promise to continue investing long-term in the Stock Market and will do all my best to take action to any other kind of investment and business opportunity while working abroad in order to become a millionaire 10 years from now for the good future of my family. I promise to continue being generous to the needy, share our blessings with others, and I will impart my knowledge. I'll be more active on building my assets portfolios from now on till I reach my definite goals in life.

Please help me, God.

Name and Signature: Jesus G. Pedines Jr.

I decided not to show you my Goal 'Passive Income Cash-flow' 5-10 year from now for a personal reason. I hope that I will be able to share that with you on my next book.

Now, don't you like to make similar promises for yourself? If your answer is yes, use the blank space below and write down your promises for yourself.

_____

_____

_____

_____

_____

_____

_____

_____

_____

_____

_____

_____

_____

_____

_____

Your Name and Signature here: _____

The promise notes you have written above is only the beginning. This will be your contract to yourself to build or rebuilt your personal philosophy. This time you got to be serious about it. If you really want to see a tremendous change in your life, if you want to achieve your goals, whatever it is, no matter how many you have listed in your diary, do it with all your heart, with all your strength, pray for it, and be happy with it.

After reading this book, you may consider finding your personal mentor to make things easy for you and find what is working for you based on the testimony or statement of those many successful people on earth. How? By reading books, watching online videos or listening to their talks. Next, if you think suit to you, then analyze and process them to create your own plan, or you may just follow those if you want to or you may innovate or improve the formula if you have a better plan or plans. They said that if we activate the right brain so that it works in conjunction with our left-brain, we can unlock powerful thought processes and creative thinking to help us multiply our outcome five times over. So, that means we can do more and can create more options. We can resolve complicated problems once we utilize that part of the brain. How? Practice it; study the procedure by reading books. Perhaps, if we haven't regularly used that portion of the brain, it may slow down or lessen the results of whatever activities we are doing. So, what do we do? Once again, practice and use it, seek for advice, look for a mentor, try again and again to enhance that part of our brain.

Indeed, I think it is true because it is happening to me. If you follow this simple instruction, time will come; the right thoughts, the right plan, and the right opportunity will come in your way, for sure you will not think twice to grab any opportunity if you do have the right tool and right mindset. What you just need to do now is to learn how to have that "mindset" and have the patient to learn how to benefit from it.

Don't stop! Always be improving, Jim Rohn said, "Don't wish it were easier, wish you were better." Learn to work more for yourself, always look for an opportunity to improve your skills, enhance your knowledge and persistence in taking action as per your plan, if the plan isn't working, don't stop - do it again, re-do the plan and try it again.

Do you know why you bought this book? It was your brain telling you to purchase this book because you think that you may learn something in this book. But the truth is because you have a good mindset to learn, which triggers your desire to take action, that is why you are now reading this book. On the other hand, some people hate reading because they weren't ready, it wasn't their priority to read and study, their desire to learn new things specifically about investing subject was very little or maybe nothing at all.

If you don't make the action after reading this book and you won't start changing your philosophy in life, here is my question; when will you take action? As I said, this book may open up your mind regarding investing in the Stock Market. Let me show you how easy it is and at least show you how to start. To be honest, it is really difficult to do a thing if you are not mentally ready, that is why I urge you to start to set your mind and write down your goals in life, and you have to believe in them.

You have to trust yourself that you can be able to deliver all required action needed in order to see results. It is okay if you will not make it in the first time, all of us fail in our first baby steps. So, I hope at least when you are in the middle of this book, you will feel better and may gradually improve your personal philosophy in life and eventually change your mindset into a higher level of thinking and behavior on taking action on what needs to be done. I am sure that when you do this, you will see miracles in your life because you are gradually reprogramming your brain to be financially literate and become a millionaire someday.

Note: I think it's good idea providing you more black space or 'take note area' for you to write on. I do believe that while you're reading this simple book ideas may pop up in your mind. So, in this way, no need for you to take piece of paper to write on.

Note No1:

_____

_____

_____

_____

_____

_____

_____

_____

_____

_____

How Did I Learn About Stock Market?

As I mentioned, it was started when I attended a presentation about financial management, then followed by reading books and then I played the online game of Robert Kiyosaki the "Rat Race" until I came across with TrulyRichClub member video on the YouTube. If I am not mistaken, he should be my upper TrulyRichClub affiliate.

After three months of reading related books, playing the Rat Race, and listening to mp3 audio self-development talks, I was able to understand Stock Market through the combination of reading online and reading materials provided by brother Bo Sanchez, then I decided to open my 7-days trial with CitisecOnline or the COL Financial Group Inc.

You know what? I didn't even complete my 7-days trials and immediately opened up my COL online account. I opened a starter account for just five thousand pesos and started applying what I have learned and what brother Bo teaches us. I was also able to invite at least 7 affiliates and earn some amount just sharing with them my affiliate link.

Three months later after opening my COL account, I was able to invest around Php. 60,000.00 in the Stock Market and went up to 80K before my final exit from being OFW. I knew that I had many shortcomings or mistakes because aside from few TrulyRichClub SAM's stock recommended by brother Bo, I also had some share stocks not listed in SAM's table, and that is one of my lessons not to repeat again unless I am fully aware of the company's status and potential growth to have profit.

Nevertheless, why wasting time to analyze stocks potential growth when in fact, brother Bo and his analyst already provided us the SAM's table that guided us? What I am trying to say is that I am already a TrulyRichClub member and I have full access to see the strategic averaging method or (SAM's) table, so I don't need to analyze company anymore, though it is also important to learn the basic technical analysis.

So from now on, I will just follow the SAM's table. But of course, it is always better if you start learning about the basic technical analysis and read speculation provided or issued by financial experts like brother Bo's TrulyRichClub resources and Sir Edward Lee, reports from trusted institution like COL Financial and other trusted brokerage firm in the Philippines.

Once You Joined The TrulyRichClub

TrulyRichClub is founded by Eugenio Isabelo Tomas Reyes Sanchez Jr. or widely known as Bo Sanchez, he is a best-selling author, an entrepreneur, a preacher and lay minister in the Philippines. He is known as the "Preacher in Blue Jeans." He was born on July 11, 1966 in Caloocan city Philippines to Eugenio and Pilar Sanchez.

In TrulyRichClub, everything will be ready for you. What you just need to do is to follow instructions and read email from brother Bo's advises and email stock alerts. Aren't sounds good? Wasn't a good deal for a newbie investor? Think about it; it is your chance to be a millionaire once you retired from being an employee or even earlier. Brother Bo's 'train,' I mean just like the 'MRT train' heading to success is open ticket. Get your ticket now, be a member of TrulyRichClub, so that once you start investing in the Stock Market, you have all the tools and basic knowledge you needed prior to opening your stock market account. To me, I became a TrulyRichClub prior to open my COL account.

If you want to start generating profits and become a millionaire before you retire from being an employee as fast as possible, make sure to be a TrulyRichClub member and take advantage of brother Bo's offers once you become a TrulyRichClub member.

TrulyRichClub members and the whole TrulyRichClub family will be available to answer your questions once you have joined the community, and gradually you will be fully equipped of all knowledge you need while on your way investing in the Stock Market to become a millionaire someday. To me, I have declared already that I will be like them 'a TrulyRichClub millionaire members' by my 40th birthday on November 27, I mean this year 2017. God willing.

Remember, if you miss this opportunity, you may find other way but it might take you time to study by yourself and remember that time is gold. For now, please make sure maintain your momentum reading this book all the way till the last page because I will be sharing more important lessons that you need to know.

Note No. 2

_____

_____

_____

_____

_____

_____

Reading Books Become my Hobby

Reading books became my hobby in 2013. Indeed, after reading the "Think and Grow Rich" by Napoleon Hill, it helped me a lot not only in my profession as a safety professional, but also in many other aspects of my life. I would say, I improved myself tremendously, my faith, my persistence to accomplish things, and my mind setting, my skills related to my profession, and even my investing skills. Have you read that book, "Think and Grow Rich?" I hope you will read it. If you're curious about what I am saying, grab a copy of that book "Think and Grow Rich" and find out yourself the success formula.

Two months before resigning from my stable job as a safety professional in Saudi Arabia in the year 2013, every day I was addicted to reading and listening to audiobook of the 'Think and Grow Rich.' Throughout the year of being a full-time businessman from mid of 2013 up to October 2014, I never stopped reading the amazing formula taught by Napoleon Hill in his book. If you read his book, you may recall what I am saying. You know what? Until now, I am still reading Hill's book and this time I am reading the Law of Success.

Yes! I did that. Imagine in just one year I feel that the formula is already within me and became part of the working element of my subconscious mind. I am telling you; this is what I feel in everything I do. Now I am more sincere on achieving any goal.

Yes, it is not easy to master the formula if you aren't willing to learn. Actually, by applying the formula on reading and studying activities, later on, you will say "I got it."

You know what? I discovered that most of my mentors have read Hill's book. They apply the formula in different approach, different strategies, especially in the world of invention, investing, businesses and many other aspects of life. Yes, if you were once aware of the Hill's formula, you will come to know that the Hill's formula remain on the top; that makes them successful.

Some of them mention this book when they are sharing their success with others, and some don't. They all become successful and wealthy because they apply the formula. However, you know what? All of us have a chance to be successful, just don't be like those people who never attempt to be successful; to those individual who easily quit and surrendered when they face challenges; to those who never learn from their mentor, and to those individual who always chose to play safe to avoid the risk. Why? Because they are afraid of failing, they are afraid to be broke, they are afraid to be criticized and afraid to lose their money, and so on and so forth.

Well, now I am proud to say that I am not that kind of individual anymore. Now I have changed, I believe that I already belong to the two percent of people on earth having a positivity mindset, at least the mindset for now; a mindset of how to create our own money making machine and a mindset to reach our goal no matter how many tough challenges along our way.

I will do all my best to master how to run our machine to make money. Someday I will become a generous wealthy investor.

I will become a mentor of my co safety professional or to those newbie entrepreneur/investors/author in my own special way.

To me, Brother Bo is one in a million mentor that many will benefit from if one just follows his advice like what he did following his mentors. Thank you brother Bo Sanchez for being my mentor.

I still remember our baby steps being an entrepreneur during our 1st year of learning on 2013. I don't forget my hobby planting vegetable in front of our house so that we can harvest free vegetable when we would like to eat vegetable. I raised broiler chicken and managed small sari-sari store to maintain and provide our kitchen supplies. In addition, you know what? The formula was working in doing such small goals, even little things. Indeed, we benefited from doing it. It helps us to survive running a small family.

Thank you to a friend who extended his support and fully trusted us lending some cash when we were shortage of money. Though, we will never know if our business partnership would have been successful or not, throughout the duration of the business, he never turned us down. Instead, he was there for us till I decided to shut-down our businesses and return to him the 30% of his total share and paid him off all my liabilities. Thank you very much, partner, for being that kind and so generous to us. May God help you to be successful with all your plans in life....

_____

_____

_____

_____

_____

_____

Retire Millionaire Investing in the Stock Market

Being a millionaire is a dream of many people like me but only few individuals are able to manage and get what they dreamed of. Many were able to achieve their goal and become a millionaire managing their own financial future. "How did they do that?" That is the usual question of those who attempted to do but never made any effort or failed to take any action.

When I started writing this book, to be honest with you, though I am earning a very stable income for living, I don't have that million pesos investment in the stock market yet; we don't have that sufficient emergency fund yet.

On July 2016, we were only able to have at least six-digit investment in the stock market when my wife and I set our goal to improve saving for our emergency fund. All of you who are reading this book will be my witness about my next goal, a challenging goal for my family. Yes! My goal is to have investments worth millions in the stock market on or before my 40th birthday on November 2017.

May God help us to manage our financial future through investing in the stock market and other assets we currently have.

So how is that? Do you know who taught me this? Yes, my mentors.

Just for sharing and for challenge purposes, I want to give you an idea why it takes me so long to have that million investments in the Stock Market wherein I am earning much monthly income from being an OFW. First of all, I am a little bit late to learn about investing, about TrulyRichClub and about Stock Market. That was on 2013, six months after attending that seminar at Riyadh Saudi Arabia followed by reading the 'Rich Dad Poor Dad' written by Robert Kiyosaki in which took me to search Philippines Stock Market that lead me to a link to watch a YouTube video about TrulyRichClub teaching viewers on how to invest in the Philippine Stock Market.

Within the same month after reading just the free materials given by Brother Bo Sanchez, I felt comfortable to be a member of TrulyRichClub. To continue the story, in few months, we were able to invest seven digits around 80K pesos in the Stock Market and got so excited. However, because of too much excitement and eagerness to mind our own business, I resigned my position as

Safety Advisor, went home back in Baguio City Philippines, and started our first five small traditional businesses.

My mentors said that being broke is only temporary and anyone has the right to rise again, again, and again until you succeed.

While learning the formula, I became more determined on everything I do. I said to myself, "I should do it, I could do it, and I will do it. Then I pray for it.

We put up a small sari-sari store in front of our house; my wife managed a salon and herbal medicine franchise center. I managed a welding shop and fabrication of decorative cornice made of plaster of Paris.

Many of my relatives and colleagues criticized my decision why I gave up my stable job earning at least 200K a month being Safety Advisor of the biggest oil and gas company in the world the Saudi Aramco in Saudi Arabia. Well, I said, "I have to manage my own business," I have to try my wings, I have to experience how to be broke, and I have to try how to run my family without expecting any monthly paycheck. I have to start a business to start learning the lesson. You know what? Robert Kiyosaki said, "If you fail fast you will learn fast." I don't mean or would say you have to do what we did. My personal reason why we decided to put up five small businesses at the same time is to learn the system fast. I decided to fast-track lessons in managing the traditional business by putting up five businesses at the same time. In the beginning, my wife didn't understand my point but when we started learning the lesson, eventually she was able to appreciate my idea, to learn how to manage our own business and to improve our skill solving business problem and difficulties.

Having five traditional small businesses in our level of experience during those days wasn't easy. For the whole year, we run the businesses and survive for a living. This experience we had was very challenging, and priceless. It gave us extreme pressure to learn lessons. If we chose to start a single small business, our income might not be sufficient to run our family considering that we are still in the transition in lowering our expenses. As I've said, I don't say or wouldn't recommend to anybody to try what we did because we have different mindset and capacity, you may have a better approach than we do. Then so be it... My advice is, take all advices from your mentors, process it and act according to your best judgment. Right now, I would say I already possess the most important formula to become wealthy in the near future, yes, the "millionaire mindset."

From having many expenses, my wife reduce our monthly budget from 50K to 15K a month. It was amazing lessons. Though I know that my family may complain, but thank God we made it.

For one year, we were able to survive. Approximate tuition fee for our learning process just to study the basic knowledge of being an entrepreneur was about Php. 600, 000.00. In return for the amount we've spent to run the business, including credits and losses of capital, we have learned many things. It may sound risky to you, but as I've said, we may have different approach and mindset to apply the formula. The good thing about this is the experience we had taught my wife how to handle a small business; we learned how to manage employees, we experienced many business difficulties (e.g. taxes, permit, employee salary and material shortage, employees cash advances, credit, shop rent, etc.). On the positive side, it helps us to enhance our financial IQ and problem solving skills and not only that, this time we spend wiser and we're learning the millionaire mindset.

Note No. 4

_____
_____
_____
_____
_____
_____

My Baby Steps in the Stock Market

Brother Bo encourages all TrulyRichClub members to invest long term in the Stock Market and not to be worried about the fact that 85% of active trader lose money in Stock Market. Why? Yes because we're not traders, we are TrulyRichClub member are long-term investors.   Brother Bo promised to all TrulyRichClub Members that he would teach us how to invest in the Stock Market through his sixteen gigantic big blessings once you become a TrulyRichClub Member. Personally, I believed in brother Bo, that's why I joined the club. By following his advice, someday I'll be able to create my millions for the future of my family. As I've said, I wrote this book to serve as my guide to attaining my goal to have investments that worth millions portfolios in the Stock Market. Brother Bo's Maid did it, so can I, and you can too. Right? It is just a matter of goal setting, correct mindset, and a burning desire to achieve that goal.

Can you imagine, brother Bo gave a 'Sixteen Big Blessings' to all TrulyRichClub active members? The only thing we need to do is to apply what he told us to do following the SAM's table, read his books and email, watch his videos, join the TrulyRichClub Facebook community or group and so on and so forth. My two favorite big blessing from brother Bo is the blessing no. 8, in which all TrulyRichClub members have a chance to earn passive income by being brother Bo's Affiliate in the TrulyRichClub. By just inviting your friends who wish to become a TrulyRichClub member, you will get a 20% commission from their monthly or annual subscription and another 5% if your friend also invited someone and joined the club. The other big blessing that I like most is the no. 11, which is the FREE Php. 100, 000.00 life insurance for those TrulyRichClub who pay a 1 year membership or subscription or have been 1 year member of the club, it means as long as you have maintained your membership, you are illegible for that FREE 100K life insurance. What a gigantic blessing from brother Bo Sanchez, isn't it? All of the sixteen big blessings are really huge gifts to all TrulyRichClub members, so we have to maintain our membership, read and use those tools to benefit from it.

It is not too late for me; I am only 38 years old turning 39 when I started writing this book. Unfortunately, I was a little bit late knowing about brother Bo TrulyRichClub. Though we are able to own a house in Baguio City in 2009 which cost us now around 4 million pesos, now I understand that a house wasn't an asset instead it is a liability. Imagine since year 2007 when I joined the Saudi Aramco Project Management Team in Saudi Arabia as Safety Advisor, we focus on building our house, at least we have our own house now. If I just knew earlier about investing in the 'Stock Market money making machine, or if I get a chance to read the book of Napoleon Hill and Robert Kiyosaki after graduation in college in the year 2001 and been a member of TrulyRichClub early on, I would say 'maybe I am a millionaire this time.' However, as I said, we're not too late, we still have a chance to be a millionaire. It's only 3 years since I'm aware of such investment. I declare in my original plan, which was written on the middle of 2013, mentioning by the end of the year 2018, I will be a millionaire. I knew myself and this time December 25, 2016, I already have proved that the formula is working. So, it is not hard anymore for me to set such goal, though this is very small amount to someone else.

Ten years ago, perhaps it might be difficult for me to think and set a goal like this because no one taught or shared with me the type of experience I am telling you now in this book. Yes, it is true that we need to work hard, save money to build our own house, to own a vehicle, to have new gadgets, and save for the kid's education. But to me, I am happy to say that I am different now. I am now on the level of mastering the millionaire mindset. I promised myself that I would never stop until I reach or achieve our goals in life at the 80% of it; "*habang may buhay may pag-asa; kung may itinanim may aanihin; kung may tyaga may nilaga*." Those Filipino sayings are really true and I am currently mastering the formula to make my dream come true. God willing.

Brother Bo advices are very simple, he said, "Just invest 20% of your salary each month into any kind of investment like in the Stock Market. Then just follow Bo's advices, which company to buy, when to sell, when and which companies to switch when needed, when to hold and stop buying. All of these questions have been addressed through the online SAM's table and stocks update from brother Bo's email. That is it, as simple as that. No need to become a financial expert. Knowing the basic will be sufficient for us being a newbie. You know what? I trust SAM's table, that is it, and I am a long-term investor.

We all know that the real secret for being successful is time. The earlier you started investing in the stock market, the wealthier you become if you are following the right system. Jim Rohn said, *don't set your goals too low. If you don't need much, you won't become much; don't wish for less problems wish for more skills. Don't wish for less challenge wish for more wisdom.*

Those quotes above from Jim Rohn opened my eye in the world of personal development. Jim Rohn also said that success is a 'number-game'- like how much you want to have in your savings, and investment, how many books you have read, how many training you needed and should attend and so on and so forth.

Okay stop for a while and try to browse Jim Rohn on the YouTube. If you can follow my basic instruction, it will be beneficial to you someday, trust me, Jim Rohn may help you open your mind to change your philosophy in life.

Mentors

Always review your performance and persistence in performing your plan; read your reasons regularly, it's okay to experience failures because failing is the key to success, so learn the lessons from those failures you've experienced then pray for it and do your best to do it right the second time executing your plans. Prepare new plans if needed as Robert Kiyosaki says, "If you've failed, that means you're doing something, and if you are doing something, you have a chance." I would love to encourage you also to purchase any book of Robert Kiyosaki. Those books may help to level up your mindset as well.

There is a lot of advice from Mr. Kiyosaki that we've tried. In my personal experience, after reading some of his books, I made my plan to retire early, and it pushed me also to keep working hard and read more books to level up my mindset and eventually pushed me to resign from being an employee on 2013. As I've said, we started our five traditional businesses in the mid of 2013, just to learn how to fail and to be broke. We know that being broke is a part of the process that we need to experience and look forward to being better investor or entrepreneurs in the near future.

Later on, we came to realize and understand the difference between assets and liabilities after reading the 'Rich Dad Poor Dad' authored by Robert Kiyosaki. Since then, my wife and I understand that a house where we live wasn't an investment rather it is a liability because it takes money out of our pocket. Just like owning a personal car, and buying expensive appliances and gadgets, those are all kinds of liabilities NOT an asset. Sounds familiar? Yes because Kiyosaki is one of my mentors. Is he your mentor too?

I would suggest you to read some book authored by the current US President Donald Trump; his 'Think Big' is one of my favorite book that makes me create a Science Fiction noble. Yes, it sounds crazy, but yes, I did it and was able to publish that book.

So far, all books that I've read about self-help and personal development were having similarities, though they have uniqueness and differences from each other, but it really does help people like me struggling to learn the secret of a wealthy person.

Mentors usually open the door of opportunity for their students or readers. They are meant to teach their mentee and provide them guidance, wisdom, advice, encouragement, ideas, skills, and so on and so forth.

Yes, when you read many books, if you don't take action and refuse to do your part, then it will be useless because you didn't even try to take any action. I hope you're not that kind of person because right now you are reading this book.

Sometimes it's so hard to convince people, but as I said, I would never stop saying this - never stop spreading any good news or opportunity to others. Learn to be a mentor and teach other people around you and keep thinking about how you can contribute to help other people in your own personal way no matter how small it is. Never give up, don't stop learning, trust yourself, you can do it.

Note No. 5

_____

_____

_____

_____

_____

_____

Imagination

All right, let us have another exercise. How open do you practice or use your imagination? According to Napoleon Hill, this is the fifth step toward success. For the sake of learning, I would suggest you to use your imagination and write down all good ideas while reading the remaining pages of this book in order for you to exercise your imagination.

Now, I will ask you this. What are those things you're imagining right now? Are they positive things or negative things? Were they good or bad ideas? Would you try to list them down in the space below?

Come on you can do it….

_____

_____

_____

_____

_____

_____

_____

_____

_____

_____

I hope you wrote something…. If so, congratulation! We are moving forward… Job well done.

You have to be cautious of what you're thinking or imagining. Here are some more following questions; what would you do after imagining those things? Did you do something about it or you've just ignored them? If we follow the formula, it could and will give you a positive result.   However,   once   you refuse to follow the formula, you may get a negative result. That is it.

Now let us go back to our exercise. Once again, stop for a while close your eyes and let us try to imagine and think about this…. How does it feel if you have millions investment in the stock market?

Please write down again…. From your imagination, how do you feel knowing that you have million pesos invested in the stock market?

_____

_____

_____

_____

_____

_____

_____

_____

_____

_____

You don't need to tell anyone how it feels. Just be honest to yourself about what you feel. It could be ridiculous feeling, there are so many negative thoughts, you may feel crazy, you may think it's impossible and many other negative emotion. However, you know what? There are tons of positive thought, emotions, ideas, and feeling in there. If you feel that positive emotion and feeling... congratulation! You have a chance.

If you felt all negative, it just so happens that your brain wasn't ready yet to process such brilliant ideas. Only you, but you who can determine if you can achieve such idea if you could and can turn that imagination or idea into physical reality.

I am not an expert on this topic, but I am still learning, and we know that in learning there are so many curves along our ways that we need to manage, that is why we need mentors.

All my books were just ideas, and I process it using my imagination, especially when I am in the making of my first sci-fi book; the 4000 A.D Scientist Rivalry- The Throne of Kepler Eagle.... Yes. It was really crazy, I was able to self-published it on February 2016. You know what? President Donald Trump was one of my inspirations when I was writing the manuscript because during that time I was reading his book the "Think Big." That is why I even included him in the book and named him 'Donald Big.' He is one of the main characters in the book as the President of the USA. Imagine that; I even predicted that he would win the US presidency election in November 2016... hahahaha... Indeed, he won. Congratulation Mr. President Donald Trump. I mentioned this just to give you an example. Because of imagination, I was able to create this book hoping that someday someone will see my work and make this simple story into a movie. Yes, I am Thinking Big, sounds impossible but who knows?

My dream car is a brand new SUV. Indeed, I wrote this as one of my goal imagining that I will be driving a brand new car on or before April 2018, so we have a decent service for our family and our future businesses. I don't know if this is a smart idea, but I include it as one of my goal and as a gift to my wife.

My Online Game, the "Ladder Safety Journey Game," though we failed in our first attempt at the development of this online apps safety game in which I lost U$3,000.00. Someday I will do my best to redo the plan, find better apps Developer Company and will make it sure to allocate sufficient fund to make this into reality.

My Ficus plantation, our training center, more book to publish, and real estate businesses, just to name few of my brilliant ideas. My assignment is to think and plan how to make them into reality. Yes, my creative imagination will be useful when I'm making my plans.

You know what? Because of my creative imagination, I think I can be an inventor as well. Why? Because when I participated in the Saudi Aramco innovation program, I was able to submit about 21 ideas, two out of 21 ideas have already been approved for implementation. When I received a notification that my two ideas were approved, I just said to myself... Wow!!! Yes! I did it again... the formula really works, we just need to stretch our capabilities or put pressure on ourselves on challenging ideas and situation.

Mindset and Goal Setting

Setting goals is not that hard, but many people neglected to set their goal. They just trusted their memory instead of listing them down on paper or in their diary.

Visualizing your goals as if it's already happening is a very powerful strategy to make things happen. Many successful people in the field of science, medicine, engineering, invention, business, arts, sports, innovation, politics, technology, and many other aspects of life were using the visualization technique before they were able to put into action and turned ideas into reality. In my experience, yes, I used to do similar strategy, I learned how to visualize things, I level up pushing the limit and do all my best to get out from my comfort zone think outside the box in order to be a stronger and better person. I became a better husband to my wife and more loving father of my kids; I turn myself into more energetic employee and better colleagues, a better son, and brother. In addition, I become more productive in everything I do as an investor, entrepreneur, and an author, as well as a safety professional.

A good mindset is significant when setting goals. Mentors, for instance, need inspiration to be successful in what they are doing. Therefore, as a newbie or mentee, we needed to follow or learn from our mentors or coach to be similar or better than them if we could.

Now, just for sharing, my inspiration is my family, they were the reason why I needed to work hard, thinking all possible income resources, using my talents and skills is one of my strategies right now to fast track investing and to achieve all my goals in life.

Any goals can be achieved as long as you stay focused on attaining that goal, any goal. Trust your guts and instinct, trust yourself and have faith in yourself that you can do it; develop your interests to learn new things; love what you do and do what makes you happy. Always do your best and maintain your momentum on initiating your plan. Yes, it is essential to develop a plan or plans and execute them not only today or tomorrow but do it every day until you succeed. Set your goals now and start working toward achieving them or else nothing will happen, they will just remain a dream that will never come true because you haven't tried to do something. It is your choice anyway, whether you will achieve that goal or just watch someone else achieving his or her goal, and you will just tell to yourself "*sayang, sana ginawa ko rin yon; sayang na sayang talaga.*"

Your dream will come true, just try and try. Yes, it is true, many were dreaming of being successful, but many didn't make it.

After being broke and experiencing one or two failure of what they are doing, they stop and never attempt to try again while murmuring "**sayang lang ang pagod ko dito, tama na, ayaw ko na, suko na ako**."

Would you think, if a person is always saying such words, do they have a chance to be successful?

Look, let us see the other side, how can an individual be so successful and enjoying their stable job while investing in the stock market and eventually retired early from being an employee and now manage their own businesses? Yes, this is the fact, because they did something, they try and try until they were able to get what they wanted. They maintain a positive attitude, study the know-how, they joined a club or group, and they attended trainings, read books and many more. I do believe that I am now heading on the same pathway. How about you?

Do you know that setting a definite goal will help you fulfill your plan? Once again, a statement of your definite goal needs to be written, so write down a statement about your goal, about who you want to become someday and what you need to do to achieve them. Make it a habit to read it aloud every day until you memorize them, sooner or later it will become a part of your daily routine especially when reading your statement emotionally with strong faith that you can do it.

When you are doing that exercise every day, and included them in your prayers, later on, you may create ideas about how to acquire that goal. Once related ideas pop up in your mind, once again, write them down quickly in your planner or notebook, so that you won't miss them, then from those ideas, you may be able to generate a plan to start with.

Now let us go back to my main topic. Why am I encouraging you to invest in the Stock Market? Let us have another exercise. Would you mind doing it again?

If your answer is no, then list down all your definite **goals and reasons** why you want to invest for your future and not just saving all your money in the bank or keep buying liabilities. The space below is provided for your use. Take your time to think about it before you proceed.

My definite goals in life are….

1. _____

2. _____

3. _____

4. _____

5. _____

My reasons why I need to start investing are….

1. _____

2. _____

3. _____

4. _____

5. _____

Always remember your reasons. Those reasons you listed will be your inspiration to attain your goal, so you may include them in your prayers. Sometimes, opportunity is already in front of you but you fail or ignore those opportunities or you may be able to notice but you can't do anything because your mindset is not yet ready or you lack self-confidence—that's why you pass or ignore on opportunities even though you'd have loved to try.

Setting a big dream, thinking big is also a proven approach to attaining goals. Your *desire* to be a millionaire for instance will be like your transportation or vehicle to attain your goals, and your *reasons* will be like your gasoline or like your fully charged battery to push you beyond the boundaries and keep you going to reach your destination successfully.

If you are currently working but don't have sufficient extra cash to invest, then you need to find ways to start investing. First, you need to re-channel your mindset, focus on clearing all your liabilities or credit, start saving for emergency fund then you may start investing little by little. If you are currently jobless, then you have to program your mind to find one; investing your time on studying on how to start investing while looking for a job is a good start or good idea.

Sometimes it seems like no one cares about your goals especially if you tell someone that you will be a millionaire someday. Some people might react negatively, which may discourage or embarrass you, and the problem is once you entertain such feedback you will not reach your destination successfully. As I've said, just ignore those NEGA people; they'll not help you. Don't be affected by what they've said. Instead, use it as a challenge. Yes, you can make it; you can achieve such goal, just follow the proven formula and join a good system.

If you can't find someone to teach you personally, at least you have to find ways to read self-help books as a guide or watch them online. If you are really serious about seeing changes in your life, you need a coach; we all need mentors to guide us, to inspire us, and to show us the way. In addition, I am telling you, a book may do. Try to read books of brother Bo Sanchez or Chinkee Tan and be inspired.

For those who haven't graduated college or are just elementary or high school graduates and don't have any experience in investing in the Philippines Stock Market, just maintain your desire and finish reading this book. Do not say it's impossible because nothing is impossible.

For those who are ahead of me, reading this book may provide you some information that could help you to fulfill your remaining plan in life.

If you've failed once, don't stop. Brother Bo said, "The secret of success – Don't stop Planting," indeed this is true, so you have to try again and again and pray for it to have good fruits when it's time to harvest. Look at Thomas Edison, he didn't stop until he was able to succeed in what he wanted. He said, "I have not failed. I've just found ten thousand ways that won't work."

Note No. 6

_____
_____
_____
_____
_____
_____

This Time I Will do it Better

As I've said, the moment you decided to purchase this book, indeed you possess the desire to level up your financial IQ and financial status.

No worries, you already possess the most important thing; the 50% secret because you have reached reading this book this far. I would say if someone doesn't possess a positive attitude even reading the introduction of this simple book would be difficult for him or her. Probably, he or she would prefer to watch movies rather than reading books like this.

For those newbies, after reading this book, your skills and knowledge to financial freedom will improve. You will learn why rich people become richer.

Yes, to tell you the truth, I haven't been there yet but I can feel and can see myself ten years from now I will attain at least 80 % of my goals in life and become financially free if God wills. All I have now is my multimillionaire state of mind as Napoleon Hill said, "State of mind is the beginning of riches."

I would say, the asset we only have right now is our positive mindset and the white heat of desire to attain our goals.   My wife and I learned to start minding our own small businesses and now focusing ourselves on creating more assets. We keep thinking options to resolve financial challenges and being not afraid to experience failure or being broke. Having an intellectual asset and regular exercising of our synthetic and creative imagination will be sufficient for now. Later on, we will be able to create our own money making machine by following the proven formula used by many successful people.

If we really want to attain the level of being financially free, therefore, we need to learn to follow a right system and secret of a successful person.

Once again, if the 'Maid' of brother Bo Sanchez can, so can you and I too, right? I loved to repeat and repeat this challenges again and again. I feel cool saying this to myself as a challenge. How about you? Try to say it to yourself with sincerity.

This is the right moment whether you're financially ready or not; the most important thing is you are mentally ready. Set your mind to enter the world of investing whether in the Stock Market, bonds, mutual funds, and real estate or putting your own business, make sure you love what you do and money will follow, just follow the formula and a good system.

Remember that you have to understand all advices and wisdom throughout the book. All exercises or instruction is essential for you to accomplish if you're really keen to change your personal philosophy and mindset.

If you have already started investing in the stock market, or you already did it in the past, well, that is better because you are ahead of other people who have zero knowledge about investing. In just very little patience, you will eventually experience the feeling of being financially free at least the feeling once you decided to try again.

To those who have zero knowledge, it doesn't matter if you do not have any experience in the world of investing right now. All that matters is that you are now reading this book and after you finish you will be ready to take your first baby steps to financial freedom.

To those ahead of me, you might be more expert or more successful than I do, I would like to thank you for spending time reading this book.

Now, let me continue sharing with you about our experience, how my wife and I changed and boosted up our mindset in the subject of financial freedom. I will show you the best I can on how we attained the level of positive mindset in order to start and get on the track of being financially free.

I started with nothing but a big desire; we don't have much capital to start our own business. That is the only one big thing I have in possession. Thinking that I can do it, I have to try; there are no excuses. I have to do it and try my wings.

This time I am not afraid of failing and I have to experience how to fail faster in order to learn fast. Our way into the world of being an entrepreneur is not easy, as well in the part of my wife when I convinced her to agree on my plan. Indeed, we had very basic technical knowledge, very little experience, and very little skills of what we were about to do.

However, we became aware of the top secret of a successful person and started leveraging our learning process by using Internet and Google, reading more books to inspire us and to learn from it. We attended several seminars to boost-up our interest and determination to pursue our goal.

Three years ago, my wife and I started our own business on the middle of 2013. We experienced so many things after struggling for one and half years managing 5 small businesses in the Philippines. Finally, we decided to try the second level.

Within just a few month of the 1st quarter of 2015, I was able to complete one of my visions to create a manuscript and publish my first book the "Think and Become Safety Practitioner" and start earning passive income from it even in very little amount. My book is now available around the world online, and I am in the process of writing more books. This book is my 4th book.

I know this journey will be challenging and not easy to face learning curves, ups, and downs along our way. However, I trust myself, I have faith that I can do it, I can now see myself earning 5 to 10 Million passive income annually by the year 2020, "God wills."

Note No. 7

_____
_____
_____
_____
_____
_____

Don't Procrastinate...We can do it!

Making Money

Before we begin in this lesson, I want to reiterate that this book is an invitation that could change your life. Maybe some people will say that it isn't appropriate for me to write a book like this, but to be honest with you, I don't care about criticism from other people, though I accepted that I am not yet that so successful on what I am propagating or advocating. What I know is that I am very committed to sharing with you what I am experiencing.

You may start listing down your own goal while reading this book or after you finish reading this book. I really wish you to feel what I am feeling right now. Once again, that feeling is the starting point. Because of my desire to share with you what I am experiencing, I have invested a lot of my time creating this book just to give you some amazing ideas and inspiration that you may have missed or ignored in the past. Having said that, I hope you will find me sincere because I believe that you're really sincere too to see changes in your life since you reach this far reading this book. Thank you for reading this book.

Now let us talk about investing for our kids. Are you aware that even our kids can invest in the Stock Market? If kids are below 18 years old, then parent's consent is needed through ITF accounts. So if we would like to see our kids be a millionaire before they reach 40, we have to start investing share stock of many profitable companies in the Stock Market for them under your account, or we may open an ITF account for them, then we need to follow a right and a proven system like TrulyRichClub system. We will just need to sell some of our kid's stocks once brother Bo advise us to sell shares or once a target selling price have reached per the SAM table. That is it, isn't that so easy to follow?

However, someone may ask. "How would I start investing in the Stock Market if I don't even have sufficient cash to pay my TrulyRichClub subscription or membership fee?"

The question above is the usual excuses of those unfortunate 'kababayan' who don't have enough or extra money to invest. Well, I think if you are able to purchase this book, it means you are one of a kind. In fact, you have already invested your time reading this book by aiming to learn something. If you can't save some money from your income, find an extra job available out there.

Use your talent or skills to earn some cash; you may join multi-level-marketing (MLM), you may accept students for tutorial or training, learn how to earn online. As I said, don't worry, money will follow, once again the first step that you must have is that mindset and a desire to invest and to be a Millionaire someday. How? Follow the formula and your plans, if your plans didn't work out, make another plan, re-do it again, use your brain and your imagination to create a new plan, and a new strategy.

I would strongly recommend you to be a TrulyRichClub member in order to build your solid knowledge or foundation in the world of investing. We know that investing in the stock market is not recommended if you don't understand how investors are making money in the Stock Market and or haven't sought for advice from a financial expert. In TrulyRichClub, everything you need to know will be provided, I would say even an individual who has ZERO knowledge about stock market, you will be guided very well by brother Bo's system.

Since I was a kid, I've been a good salesman and a business-minded youngster, but imagine I just started listing my goals in life on 2013, though in the past I was just thinking about them. Since then, I learn and dream to mind our own business and start learning how to invest in the Stock Market. I think I am lucky to have a positive feeling that "I am not too late to achieve my goal in life."

You might question why I keep repeating some of my statement and self-promises in this book. Once again, I come up with this book because this book will be my guide and will serve as an extension of my personal contract to accomplish my entire goal as much as I can; at the same time, I may provide guidance to our '*kababayans*' like you at least showing you the way to success. At least, I did something to help people.

By sharing my goals with you, you will be a living witness of my success, "God willing." Now, I want to share with you my top goals listed in my diary

First in my list, I have written this year 2017, that I'll become a millionaire on my 40th birthday. Secondly, I'll be the CEO my own company on 2019. I also listed or dream to own the biggest supplier of Ficus Elastica plant in the Philippines. How is that?

How about being an author of at least 20 books by the year 2020.

On 2016, I will treat my family to a tour in Hong Kong Disney Land. Thank God this was already accomplished.

On 2018, our family house will be fully furnished and will be titled while constructing our training center building and should be completed by the end of 2019.

My wife said, "make it sure, you will have in-place that million on your 40th birthday on 2017," and I sincerely replied, "I think we can make it honey with your help." God willing.

On 2019, we will start traveling all over the Philippines visiting universities and colleges promoting my books.

By 2020, I should be earning at least 5 million to-10 million pesos annually. Sounds crazy? In fact, this is a very little goal to somebody. However, you know I need to set my SMART goal, which I think I can successfully deliver the required action according to my plan.

What do you think? Is it possible? Once again, there is no harm in setting goals or target. Now let's try it once again, this time you will list down what you want to achieve, what you dreamed off. Of course goals for the family is always special, to all my daughters and for my wife. Actually, all of these goals are for them, to give them a good future. I am just planting the seeds for them to harvest the fruits someday.

Remember that in investing, time is gold, if you start earlier, then the wealthier or richer you become. Just like planting a tree.

For instance, if you are just a student and your allowance is just sufficient, for your food and transportation, then during summer you have to find a summer job to start earning and start opening an account in the stock market. Alternatively, if you have a chance to save money from your allowances, I hope you will consider my advices to start minding your financial future through investing in the Stock Market and be a TRC member.

Now, on the space below write down your top-5 dream and goal in life.

_____

_____

_____

_____

_____

_____

_____

_____

Your goals that you have written above can be your inspirations to study well to get a good stable job. After you have graduated from college, enable you to fast truck funding your Stock Market investment.

When I learned about Internet Marketing, I started managing my own website, yes I am spending money to maintain my own website though I am not earning yet from it, some people may say I am just wasting money, but my reason is to learn. I said, someday I will benefit from it.

I hope this time you already understand what I am sharing and teaching you. In the coming pages, I will tell you some more about a wonderful discovery about myself. A very simple habit may completely change my life. I think when you will do the same, your dream will come true. It might sound a bit crazy to believe, but look at me, I never dreamed of becoming an author, but here I am, now you are reading my fourth book. Believe me, the formula is working.

This time all I ask is that you have to read this book all the way down to the last page and follow the 10 basic steps below.

Note No. 8

_____
_____
_____

Don't Procrastinate...We can do it!

_____

_____

_____

10 Simple Steps

1. Be a TrulyRichClub member as early as you can. I recommend annual membership to have 20% discount and avail the FREE Php. 100, 000.00 life insurance.

2. As much as possible read all material and watch/listen to the videos-mp3 modules/materials provided by TrulyRichClub to all new members. As I've said, this is one of my lessons, I forget to utilize the materials provided by brother Bo to all TrulyRichClub members. That is why I am telling you this, so that you won't forget too.

3. After reading TrulyRichClub materials, explore with YouTube and watch more videos about TrulyRichClub Strategic Averaging Method table (SAM's table) to understand it very well.

4. Once you have completed the TrulyRichClub new member modules, you can start familiarizing about COL Financial System. Try the FREE 7 day's trial of COL Financial. I am personally promoting the COL Financial Inc. since I am a TrulyRichClub member.

5. You can start promoting your affiliate link to your friends by email, Facebook, Twitter, etc. You will be learning more about the know-how of promoting your affiliate link once you have completed the new TrulyRichClub member training modules. In addition, it is really important to share your experience face to face with your colleagues and friends.

6. After that, you may open your COL Financial online account anytime. Fill out the necessary forms and submit all requirements to COL Financials. COL representative or agent will guide you from A-Z on how to open your COL account. Then start funding your account via counter deposit or online banking especially if you are an OFW. In COL Financial, you can open an account for just P5,000 as Starter, P25,000 for Regular, and P1,000,000 for Premium. Fund your account monthly and start buying companies recommended by TrulyRichClub as per the SAM's table.

7. Continue searching and leverage your time in learning via reading books, blogs, and relevant news available online. Watch YouTube video and relevant TV shows. I would recommend ANC TV shows.

8. Don't stop learning, ensure to maintain your TrulyRichClub membership, and if you have a chance plan to attend brother Bo seminar and talks, classroom training provided by COL Financial, and any other relevant training opportunity.

9. Be an active member of TrulyRichClub and join Facebook group or group of people with similar interest whom you can share your passion and try to create relationships with them to expand your network.

10. Start building your dream and managing your financial future and don't forget to help needy people. Give charity, and maintain that "generous millionaire mindsets."

When following the basic 10 steps above, take it seriously, set your goal, dedicate your time to learning, make a plan or plans and decide whether you are ready or not.

Are You Willing to Take the Risk?

Personally, I do believe that each and every one of us has a unique way to teach people around us regardless of what topic you're sharing with them. Some people also don't even bother themselves to share what they know that could help other. I am not trying to be as wealthy as my mentors, but I want to follow their ways of thinking? But who knows? Anyone can be like them. You could be more than capable and knowledgeable of being an investor than I do, but my question is. "What will you do, are you considering mentoring other people to invest in the stock market? Do you have the right mindset now? Do you know what stock market is all about, if so, then that is great because you did start learning how to take and manage the risk?" So, if your answer is YES, but hasn't started yet, start now. If your answer is NO, but want to know more, please keep reading.

Why do we need to study the benefit of investing in the stock market? Why do we need to learn how to manage the risk and start developing your passion doing things that you loved to do? Think big, don't let anyone stop you from achieving your dreams and be a millionaire someday. How is that? Sounds good, right? But if you're still in the stage of having those fear and negative thoughts, just keep your momentum in learning the system, the process, and the secrets of millionaires.

I still remember when I come across an academy online asking to join a webinar and training online that cost me a lot of money. You know what? Right away that night I registered and paid off the tuition fee because that's what my guts said. I believed that I could learn new skills from it, new things that may help me to achieve my goals someday. I didn't think about losing but winning and investing some money just to enhance my knowledge in the Internet marketing industry. After a month of training and having a lifetime access to the academy website, I tremendously improved my ability to think new ideas and enhance my skills in the online industry. I started to develop my own digital product, that's why I became an author. Thank you very much to Profit Academy by Anik Singal, though I wasn't able to make things happen as Anik dreamed for us as his student. Indeed, it helps me a lot to make other things in my own personal way to achieve my goals in life.

Never say 'NO' to good opportunity. I mean, you may say NO in some circumstances, just for strategy or delaying tactics for instance with the intention to analyze the opportunity. A good deal is a good deal any time such good deal comes across your way, but my question is; can you determine which one is good or bad deal? Being able to determine good or bad deal will lead you to avoid procrastination. If you are not sure if it is or was a good deal, instead of saying NO better to say, "I'll think about it" or just say ,"YES I'll take it." In this case, you will have time to analyze the deal or calculate the risk. However, sometimes deals seem to be a good deal but later on it turns to become a disaster or bad deal. Do some research; you may need to ask the opinions of knowledgeable people around without disclosing your reason, the deal or an idea, then you may finalize your decision with your own judgment or perception. Make it sure that whatever decision you have made whether it's low or high risk decision, you should involve your partner. Learn how to manage the risk so that in any circumstances that may happen as result of that decision you've made, you are ready, you have options to resolve issues. Considering the opinion and decision of your partner-wife or husband will eliminate any misunderstanding in the future if ever plans won't work, he/she will be your companion to create resolution and come up with new ideas to resolve problems.

Always be ready and be equipped with your backup plans just in case things go wrong, always remember your priority. I mean your ABCs, never take shortcuts. In the stock market, experts say that timing is very important. Timing when to buy and sell certain stocks. In other types of investing, for instance, if you are signing any legal documents do not just do it by yourself, you may need the assistance of your own lawyer to explain that particular legal documents. As I've said, be very cautious and wise but avoid procrastination, I mean decide quickly as fast as you can but be diligent to follow basic rules. One idea or one deal may bring you to success and happiness and make you to be a millionaire someday; or for the sake of sharing- as a challenge to myself…. Be a millionaire like me 1 year from now.

Note No. 9

_____

_____

_____

_____

_____

_____

Don't Procrastinate…We can do it!

Online Learning

Considering your knowledge and understanding capabilities on Stock Market topics if you are a newbie like me to this kind of investment, the best thing to do is to be a member of TrulyRichClub. Once you become a TrulyRichClub member and understand all necessary instruction following upon opening your COL account, you are now managing your financial future. Time will come when you will be able to understand the basic principles of investing in the stock market and developed a good attitude of being an investor. You will feel the millionaire mindset someday and become more cautious spending your money and wiser in investing in the stock market and other good deal investment available outside the stock market. You may develop your fashion to build your own digital product just like what I am doing; the proof is this book. I hope you will check my name online and visit my personal website, check my books at amazon.com, just to give you a hint of what I am telling you. Be passionate about anything that makes you happy. Think of anything that can help people, if you think that your idea can help or teach people, then you have a chance to be successful at what you want to attain in life no matter what it is. At the end of the day, being successful is to get what you want no matter how small or big it is.

Before I continue, I would like to declare that I will be donating to TrulyRichClub ministries my 50% income for every sale made by TrulyRichClub. Actually, this idea popped up in my mind after watching one video of brother Bo mentioning the opportunity to have a one million life insurance. Though it isn't yet available this time, when I was writing this book for sure I will grab this gigantic blessing once it is available for all TrulyRichClub member. I believed that this book would bring me the miracle to achieve one of my goals to help more poor people. By just sharing my journey as TrulyRichClub member and promoting the advocacy and guidance of brother Bo TrulyRichClub. By achieving, even a small goal can make you feel like a wealthy person. At least the feeling... I feel that already.

Well, I am impressed! You've reached the halfway point within this book. It is not easy to read a book if it is not your hobby. If you think this guidebook is beneficial, please don't hesitate to recommend it to your friends and relatives.

Now, let us have an exercise. If you are currently working and planning to try investing in the stock market please writing down that goal and make a plan; e.g. when you want to become a TrulyRichClub member? When are you going to open your COL account? Now take your diary or planner and write down your simple plan answering the question above.

Yes! You need to plan; you need to invest some funds from your own pocket to be a TrulyRichClub member, once you become a TrulyRichClub member, eventually you are investing very little amount to acquire that knowledge that may show you the way to becoming rich someday. Be a student of brother Bo. Indeed, brother Bo's ways of teaching is a unique one. Your access to

TrulyRichClub page will be open for you 24/7 a day to benefit the reliable SAM's stock table when buying or selling stocks.

Here is another good benefit of being a TrulyRichClub member. Do you know that once one become a member you have a chance to earn commission from inviting affiliate, and upon accessing your records you will be entitled to 100K life insurance? Wasn't that a very good opportunity and privilege?

Now, if you're presently not earning that much income, you can still start investing as low as 5,000.00 pesos and once you are ready to invest in higher level go for it. Every time you can fund your account. Don't waste your time, just make it sure that you are investing in the right time and right company in a right price. If not, you may need to wait for the right opportunity. To be safe follow TrulyRichClub SAM's table.

For those just getting started or newbie, if you have a chance to listen to the power talk offered by brother Bo, please do it. Though I have never attended Bo's training and power talks yet, I will make it sure that someday I will meet brother Bo and other co- TrulyRichClub member. Someday I will meet brother Bo in the right time and place.

As I told you, I have a burning desire to meet brother Bo someday. If you don't have the desire to do things, it will be difficult for you to make it happen. We have a saying as Filipino "Kung gusto maraming paraan at kung ayaw maraming dahilan." Brother Bo is and will be my long-term mentor for sure because I believe in his capability. What I am trying to say is that it is very important to have a mentor, to attend their trainings or at least listen to their talks through the internet, read their books, and so on and so forth.

I recommend that after completing reading this book, read once again the books of brother Bo especially the "8 Secrets of the Truly Rich and Choose to Be Wealthy." You have to read those books again and again and start mastering bro Bo's formula and build your own plan. List down all your brilliant ideas to awaken your subconscious mind and eventually enhancing your synthetic and creative imagination.

Nevertheless, if you are currently jobless, it's better for you to find a job because you really need a steady income to fund your investment account. For those currently working, you know already what to do. I have already mentioned many things, many offers, and advice from bro Bo. Make sure you act drastically but surely. I mean surely, by following a good system, a system like being a member of TrulyRichClub before starting investing in the Stock Market and following COL financial system.

For more references, use the Google online; use the technology to help you expand your knowledge; use your spare time to read and watch related videos and other related information or topics available online or TV shows. Just type the word "Philippines Stock Market or Investment." just make sure to visit only those reputable website so that you will be well guided. So, invest your time to speed up the process of gaining investment skills and knowledge. Reduce some of your usual daily habits and focus on your goals.

Learning is always good. Learn from your mentor; nourish your education, skills, and capability. Mentors always said to their mentee, don't be afraid - you can do it - trust yourself. Personally, I loved those advices and it has become my philosophy since then.

Learning or knowing the fundamentals of any subject is very important. Yes, it is true that investing in the stock market is risky as experts always said. But there are many big IF. That IF is, e.g. "IF you don't know the fundamental; IF you are not following a good and stable and reputable system and many more.

To be aware of the fundamental meaning, at least you understand the basic of Technical Analysis (TA) - the science of recording trading data of an asset with a goal of predicting the direction of a certain stock prices. To be an expert on stocks, TA could be complicated or difficult for us as a newbie, but they can be learned. Actually, once you become a TRC member, those TA is already done for you because brother Bo and his team have already done the performance TA of each company listed in the SAM's table.

Now if you have decided to buy other companies, which are not listed in the TrulyRichClub SAM's table, then this is at your own risk. I would say, be knowledgeable enough to do such action. If you are not yet ready, just follow SAM's table.

Once again, start learning the fundamental of technical analysis, trending analysis such as primary, secondary, and minor trends. To be honest, I am not yet an expert on this, but maybe someday. At least I understand the basic types of charts (e.g. Candle, Bar and Line charts, and many other charts), and lines to understand to be an effective investor like what is "support and resistance lines/level." In this way, you will benefit from those tools/references available in your COL and TrulyRichClub system.

As times go by, when you decide to buy or sell stock which is out of the SAM's table, at least you will be able to analyze trends and pattern and able to predict the direction of assets by yourself at your own risk. But the best is, in a combination of your own analysis and from the stocks update, blogs, and analysis provided by financial experts or the COL Financial and TrulyRichClub team; you may have a stronger gut when and which company to buy and sell. But right now, as I've said, let us focus and follow the amazing TrulyRichClub system.

In COL Financial, they teach us to focus on the so-called GEMSS strategies on choosing which stocks to buy.

G-rowing Industry

E-arning Visibility

M-anagement Credibility

S-uperior Products

S-trong Balance Sheet

Just like TrulyRichClub, COL also taught us the cost averaging strategy on other Blue-Chip stocks in which an investor should keep buying stocks regardless of the price, whether it is high or low, in other words, this type of investing strategy is good for a Long-Term investors.

Personal Checklist

In my other books, the "Think and Become Safety Practitioner and the second edition How to Become a Safety Practitioner," I also used this part. I decide to include this also in this book because of the relativity of the subject when making our personal checklist.

Here is my personal experience on the importance of writing and taking notes. Actually, I did improve a lot in taking notes after reading the book, "Think and Grow Rich" by Napoleon Hill. First of all, I am not a professional writer nor have I dreamed of being an author but suddenly it has become one of my habits, and now here I am developing my skill of how to write a book. Through the help of professional writers out there I know that I can improve more in my spelling, grammar, punctuation, sentence structure, tenses, and so on.

Anyhow, you don't need to be perfect or a professional writer when writing down your personal checklist, right? Whether that was at home or at your workplace. This is my habit, taking notes and if it is really important idea. I have to write them down in my planner or even in a post-it paper. In 2013, actually, my idea to start writing a book was only one item listed in my personal notes, but now this is it, you are reading my 4th book.

Maybe you are already doing it, but you are not aware of the importance of notes. For me, as long as you can understand what you have written on paper, whatever it is, it will help you to recall and will guide you to complete a certain task that needs to be done first and last. Usually, you can see those notes stuck on the walls in your office or at home on the fridge. They are helpful, right? Yes, notes do help a lot; don't trust your memory! Learn to take a note every time you have a good idea, especially when attending seminars or trainings or even when you are sitting at home, anytime anywhere whatever you're doing. You may record it using your mobile phone, save a text message and so on. The most important thing is that you have to find a time to get back, review your notes and messages, and start working on it. As my mentor said, in the afternoon or in the evening we have to review what we've listed on that day, on the weekend we have to review what we've listed throughout the week, at the end of the month we have to review what we've listed on that month and as well for the whole year. Why? Just to review and learn from it, we may miss something, we may neglect the important things, so in this way we can re-do any plan if needed. Having tons of notes will be useless if you didn't take action.

In my personal interpretation, we as individuals should have our own personal checklist to set our targets and goals, look at those successful persons, for they surely have a lot of important notes and ideas written in their diary and they did something that helped them to become successful.

Now, why do I call it a personal checklist? I want to show you how significant a checklist is so that we won't forget or miss important things. I mean personal checklist is about ourselves, plans for our family such as children's education, monthly savings, investments, number of trainings/seminar to attend, what and how many books to read, what age you are planning to retire, and when you want to be a millionaire, to have your own business, your own house, and so on.

You can list whatever target you want to achieve or want to have or to obtain as one of my mentor said, "Whatever the mind believed and conceived we can achieve." Setting targets starts from our thoughts, so it is best to write it down—once again, don't just trust your memory. Planning will follow as you regularly review your reasons and your personal checklist. Then when the plan is ready, follow your steps from A to Z as per your plan and keep your burning desire, and act right away with positive thinking.

Yes, writing down as a note is the key and making a plan is very important but needs positive action to implement them. No matter how hard it is, start now and keep going; don't quit achieving your goals. Don't be afraid of failing; learn from your own mistakes and the mistakes of others around you. Once again, if you want to study the secrets of successful people on how they were able to conquer fear and challenges and become successful people, then grab the book "Think and Grow Rich." This is such an amazing book as a guide. Indeed, it really works. I read this book several times and would love to read it again and again. For now, at least I know I have learned to have the right mindset. I can feel that I am on my way to having at least some of those secrets to being successful in what I am doing.

After you finish reading Hill's book, you will realize that my book is guided by his book to the best of my knowledge and capability linking the formula on how to guide you based in my experience in the stock market and being a TrulyRichClub member.

Note No. 10

_____
_____
_____
_____
_____
_____

Required Courage

Many people don't have the required courage in investing in the stock market though they loved and wish to try. They said and think that stock market is too risky; stock market is only for rich people. Where in fact it is true, it is risky; but it is false that it is only for rich people. Yes, it is risky if you are doing stock market without the guidance of knowledgeable financial consultant or adviser. Well, in our situation being a TrulyRichClub member, we aren't thinking that way because we trusted brother Bo's guidance.

The lack of courage, not trusting themselves, and the fear of being criticized by someone, fear of losing their money always lead one to procrastination. Usually, it's hard for them to make a decision and in most cases, they are prepared to decline on every good opportunity.

For you, since you are reading this book, you have a chance not to be like those individual, you are doing something, and you have that desire and interest to learn new things for your future, right? Someday, once you're ready to take your baby steps in investing in the stock market or any investment available out there - the formula is very simple.

Here is my thought, it doesn't matter when did you start understanding the formula of the investing - the science of moneymaking money. What matters most is that having the desire to learn the know-how and have that passion to start doing it. There are many ways to learn how to invest. The Internet itself is more than sufficient to know everything. Now I will ask you this. "Do you have sufficient courage to learn the science of investing? Are you ready to convert your dream into physical reality?

Let us do some exercise before you continue reading considering that you have an Internet connection, try to Google "Investment" and become aware of what people or companies are saying about investment. This is very simple instruction but very few individual follow such instruction because as I've said, they are lacking knowledge of the real benefit of investing in the stock market or could be totally zero interest to learn about investment. Why? Yes! Mindset differences.

Now if you're not that kind of person and if you want to fast-track learning, then the best thing for you to do is to attend the TrulyRichClub's "Quick Start Plus+ Implementation Seminar." I haven't participated in this training because when I learned about this opportunity, I was already 3 years as TrulyRichClub member and I have done my assignment learning the basic by myself; that is why it took me more time to learn the basic knowledge of how to start. I will tell you more about this lessons I have learned about the result of not utilizing those tools readily available provided by TrulyRichClub to all member.

Let us continue…. So, if you don't have much time to read and learn online, feel free to attend this seminar, apart from the refundable P200.00 reservation fee, it is FREE for TRC members -

of course, you will be spending some cash on your food and transportation to and from the venue.

I still remember when I just arrived in Saudi Arabia on 2003. One of my friend advised me about my salary, so I replied I have P25, 000.00/month; then he said, "Here in Saudi Arabia, it doesn't matter how much you're earning, what really does matter is how much you are able to save monthly and how much take home cash you have every vacation or after completion of your contract." After our conversation, I ignored the good message. Yes, literally I understood what he was saying, but not the principle behind his statement. I knew it was important, but I only understood what he really meant when I experienced the two situations of having a basic salary and earning a competitive salary.

One of my shortcoming about that statement is that I never attempted to study how to save or invest during those days; what all I know is to save in the bank. It took me at least ten years (from 2003-2013) before I finally have the eager to learn and earn from investing. To me, it wasn't that bad because my wife and I haven't wasted all our earnings to nothing because we were able to save some in the bank and build our house worth 4 million now and not yet completed…. Yes LOL!!!

With all due respect, just for sharing. There are many OFW's who got even higher salaries than me but imagine, by using a very simple mathematics since 2007 I was earning around P180, 000.00 - P200, 000.00 a month, that means from 8- 9 years earning of that much salary. I already earned more or less around

18 million pesos, and if we apply bro Bo Sanchez' calculation, supposedly, I have at least millions savings and stock portfolio this current year 2016. But as I said, this is a challenge to us, we aren't too late, and we still have a chance, right? I promised myself and my wife that we will be millionaires on or before my 40th birthdays on 2017. We should have at least 1 million investments in the stock market.

Join TrulyRichClub now. Let us achieve our Goal and be millionaires in the Stock Market.

To have 1 million pesos invested in the Philippines stock market is one of my goals right now at least a million investments rolling in the stock market as my first moneymaking machine. Imagine that goal. Do you think this is possible?

Anyone can set his or her goal right - I said to myself, few years from now, I'll be a millionaire. If I am not mistaken, I made this decision after reading the book Think and Grow Rich and listening to Jim Rohn mp3 audio.

I want to be a millionaire, I want to manage my own business, I want to travel to all beautiful places in the Philippines, and I want to have a brand new car by 2018. Saying those things to myself regularly with a sufficient courage and determination to have them soon has eventually kept me thinking and planning how I'm going to achieve those dreams.

For those who read my first book, the "Think and Become Safety Practitioner," you may recall how passionate I am with my profession. It is a similar passion I use and will do in order to achieve all my dreams or goals. I dreamed of writing a book about investing. Now this is it; you are now reading my first book about investing; before it was just an idea and eventually came to physical reality.

Now my goal on the year 2017 is to achieve a million investments in the stock market on or before my 40th birthday on 2017. It might sound crazy for those who haven't read those books that I have read, and it could be an inspiring idea to those newbies in the stock market. For those TrulyRichClub members, it could sound normal because brother Bo taught us that such idea is achievable, right?

I believed that I can achieve this goal, and that is why I am sharing it with you. Otherwise, this book will be just a book. So I think, by sharing this goal with you will serve as another form of challenge for me to push myself to take another extra mile to prove that the formula is really working and everything that we believed that we can achieve will come to physical reality. I have a different mindset now. I hope you will have that mindset soon.

I still remember prior to being aware about TrulyRichClub, I was so afraid every time I heard about stock market. I was thinking that Stock Market is only for businessman, for company manager's and CEO's and only for rich people. But because I became a member of the TrulyRichClub, I was able to overcome those fear and start digging and exploring my financial IQ by reading many books; as many, and as fast as I could.

Yes, reading book has become my bridge to learning faster about investing, authors of those books become my mentors.

Note No. 11

_____

_____

_____

_____

A Reminder

I do believe that I can help people in my simple personal way. Now I have a millionaire mindset, so at least in my imagination I have already achieved my goal. 'I do believe I have learned to see the end before the shows begin.' Imagine at this moment typing this sentence, I am saying this as a promise to myself because I already have a millionaire mindset.'

Now let's go back to our topic. This book is about sharing, right? So, let me continue discussing some more about personal development.

Remember, when we couldn't succeed in the first attempt, do not surrender no matter how many times we failed. If you surrender and never attempt to try it again, then you have accepted that you're a looser.

Make a habit to learn from your own mistakes, don't stop extending your help to the needy even though you may have the same situation as they are; give charity in your own way. Even a smile is a charity. The more charity you give, expect more blessings to come.

Now, once you get what you want, you have achieved that goal, but don't stop there just continue achieving the rest of your goal. You may set new goals to achieve. Go back to your goal list and take a look, maybe you miss something.

Sometimes when someone gets what he or she wants, they stop and lose their momentum. However, I tell you this, things may change tremendously if you don't watch your steps, if you neglect the formula you will never improve more unless you have really decided to stop, as simple as that.

Always remember the difference between asset and accountability, we should maintain focusing on buying assets so that when we earn from those assets, we can be able help more people. Don't be greedy. What is wealth if you don't share to others, to the poor or to a charity? Those are the choices and situations that you really need to face; it is up to you how you are going to live your life when you become a millionaire someday. So let us be wise on managing your assets and let us be a generous millionaire like brother Bo Sanchez.

Always remember your reasons and just keep working to overcome all the challenges along your way. You might experience many trouble and criticisms from other people or even from your own relatives, but don't be affected by those kind of people, once again you have just started your journey.

My point of view here is that it's okay to be an employee for a certain period of time. In addition, if you are happy to retire as an employee, there is nothing wrong with that. But if someday, just in case you have had the feeling or dream of owning a business or wants to start investing in the Stock Market, you may start learning now by reading books of those successful entrepreneurs and investors to inspire you and upgrade your mindset. For us, we are still in the process of mastering the formula on how to become a successful entrepreneur and investor. While working as an employee, investing at least 20% of our earnings is absolutely very important.

I encourage you to attend motivational or self-help trainings near you or watch educational-informative-encouraging TV shows or online like the ANC On the Money or, The World Tonight, Market Edge, Shoptalk, and many more. Also, do your best to find ways to attend any inspirational seminars. For us, as a TrulyRichClub member, we do have a lot of inspirational videos from brother Bo and brother Bo regularly invites us to join him every time he has an event.

Open your mind and start learning the secrets of successful individuals so that you'll be inspired too like we do.

My persistence focusing on achieving my goals led me to become successful in my profession. However, the best part was confronting those challenges with persistence and unbroken determination. We won't grow if we hadn't experienced and learned the lesson of tough situations. We have to learn from our mentors, taken the good, and thrown out what we didn't like. Just keep moving, try and try, remember your goals and reasons. If you are TrulyRichClub member, just copy exactly how and what brother Bo Sanchez told us to do, and how we can manage those situations as they arise. The more we try despite many failures, the more successful we will become.

In addition to this, I would say, "Time is gold," so we have to decide right away, the train is waiting for us to get on board to financial freedom. It is a one-way ticket to success; a brighter future for us is only around the corner, just try and always do your best with good faith and definite purpose. Stay hungry for learning new things. Don't be like those kinds of individuals who haven't tried to level up their knowledge and dream in life. Fear of being criticized by someone or even your family may be the things stopping you from doing things you wanted to do but just keep your desire to achieve your goal, never mind what they've said, and you may overcome all challenges.

Updates

December 25, 2016

Dear readers, I don't intent showing you my COL portfolios just to impress you because it isn't impressive yet. As I told you, this book is all about sharing with you my journey, sharing everything that I think could show you the way to start building your portfolios in the Stock Market with the guidance of TrulyRichClub.

Just recently, I realized a very good lesson for myself, imagine for about 3 years being a member of the TrulyRichClub I found out that I haven't completed all my module for all new TrulyRichClub member yet. I also never completed my filling up all the information needed in my TrulyRichClub account. I said to myself, "What?" Then I realized that I really did the hard way. In fact, it is already available in the TrulyRichClub member's ONLY web page. So, what I did is start taking or watching all my modules. In fact, while writing this portion of the book, I haven't completed yet all. But for sure before the end of this year 2016, I will complete all modules and make my account better in terms of filling up all required info in my TrulyRichClub personal profile. Sorry for that brother Bo. Now I have learned a very good lesson.

My COL account snapshot below was taken on July 6, 2016. I really keep saving all my transaction for these purposes specifically for this part of the book. If I am not mistaken, this was my 2nd attempt to rebuilt my portfolios when one of my affiliate shares with me his portfolios.

Action	Stock Code	Stock Name	Portfolio %	Market Price	Average Price	Total Shares	Uncommitted Shares	Market Value	Gain / Loss	%Gain/ Loss
BUY I SELL	ABS	ABS-CBN CORPORATION	9.49	47.3000	50.8316	100	100	4,673.29	-409.87	-8.06%
BUY I SELL	FNI	GLOBAL FERRONICKEL HOLDINGS	62.06	0.8800	0.8915	35,000	35,000	30,556.14	-647.35	-2.07%
BUY I SELL	MEG	MEGAWORLD CORPORATION	9.53	4.7400	3.8230	1,000	1,000	4,693.19	870.19	22.76%
BUY I SELL	MER	MANILA ELECTRIC COMPANY	18.92	313.0000	311.7170	30	30	9,315.35	-36.15	-0.39%
					TOTAL EQUITIES					49,236.97
					TOTAL EQUITIES GAIN/LOSS					-223.20
				TOTAL PORTFOLIO TRADE VALUE						49,236.97
				DAY CHANGE					0.00%	0.00
				PORTFOLIO GAIN/LOSS					-0.45%	-223.20

Your Total Account Equity Value is 49,885.99

To those TrulyRichClub members may be you will ask me why I have stock that wasn't included in SAMs table. Well, yes, that is true but I promise to my self, from now on, I'll do my best to follow brother Bo's SAMs table.

You know what? Yes, I try my best to guide all my TrulyRichClub affiliate until such time they can stand on their own. Yes! Indeed, some of my affiliates become better that me, one of them already have 500K investments while I am here just having 5K JFC in my portfolio before I restarted funding my COL account on July 2016. Yes, I keep my JFC just not to close my account. After my conversation with my affiliate, I regain my interest to renew my TrulyRichClub membership and start funding my COL account again. So this is it, I have about 50K again in my portfolios on July 6, 2016.

COL Funding Online FYI Update No.1

December 20, 2016

Here in my FYI update # 1, my objective is to show you a sample receipt when you deposit or transfer an amount to your COL account. Nothing special here, but I think it is good to share with you just FYI. Usually I am funding my COL account via online transaction, but sometime my wife also remitted some fund via counter deposit. See (*Figure 1*)

December 20, 2016

Attention: **JESUS G PEDINES JR.**

This is to acknowledge receipt of your deposit with the following details:

NV Official Acknowledgement Receipt No: **1980092**
Credited to Account No: _____
Gross Amount: **Php 13,000.00**
Bank Charges: **Php 5.00**
NET AMOUNT CREDITED TO ACCOUNT: **Php 12,995.00**

Please expect portfolio balances to reflect deposits soon after being received during the trading period. Deposits received after trading time will be reflected into your balances after the completion of the day's transactions (which could extend to the evening session during heavy transaction days).

Figure 1

Dream Come True Update N<u>o</u>.2

December 27, 2016

By the way, I am so glad to tell you this update. Actually, this idea of mine was crystalized in my mind on 2013, that is why I resigned my job, though I knew that I wasn't ready yet that time, I still insisted on going home back to the Philippines to learn new things. Yes, I trusted my guts no matter what may happen. Since that dream didn't materialize during those days, just to satisfy myself, I made a miniature building of that dream training center. See below picture (*Figure 2*). I hope someday I will be able to start managing my own training center.

Now, here is my update # 1. I am almost done with my manuscript when I received a message from a Facebook friend inviting me to deliver an inspirational talk with his student taking IOSH Managing Safely. So I said, "Yes, of course, I will be there to give a speech to your student Mr. RM... I'll be there," I said.

To make the story short, Mr. RM, the owner of the RJGM Safety Training and Consultancy became my friend. Together we shared our dreams and plans, later on, he decided and offered me a very good deal which I never expected he'd be offering such opportunity. The idea was just to promote my book after I delivered my message to his students. It seemed that my goal to have my own Safety Training Center would be near to happen. Well, while saving some cash to fund the construction of my dream-training center, I also accepted Mr. RM offer to be his partner; in this way, I can be able to start learning how to handle or run a training center.

My point here is that I want you to understand the magnet or force of an opportunity when you keep thinking and visualizing your dream, your goal or an idea how to turn in into reality. Like what I am experiencing, many opportunities are coming along my way. I hope I will learn many things with Mr. RM. I will be extending my support on his safety training and consultancy services. After two years, I believe that I would be fully equipped with all the information and skills on how to manage a training center with Mr. RM. assistance... I will be willing to learn from him.

Figure 2

Don't Procrastinate...We can do it!

TRC Member Modules Update No.3

December 29, 2016

As promise to myself, yes, I finally completed my entire module to make my TrulyRichClub member profile look good. Another goal achieved. Indeed, this is one of my mistakes; I never navigated the entire TrulyRichClub member's ONLY page. If I just utilized them right away after I became a member on 2013, maybe this time I would say I have a better portfolio in the stock market. See (*Figure 3*)

My TrulyRichClub Profile Grade

PERCENTAGE	YOUR GRADE
7%	7%
7%	7%
7%	7%
5%	5%
5%	5%
5%	5%
5%	5%
5%	5%
5%	5%
5%	5%
5%	5%
5%	5%
5%	5%
5%	5%
5%	5%
5%	5%
7%	7%
7%	7%
TOTAL	100%

Figure 3

Portfolios Flash Back Update No.4

July 6, 2016

Action	Stock Code	Stock Name	Portfolio %	Market Price	Average Price	Total Shares	Uncommitted Shares	Market Value	Gain / Loss	%Gain/ Loss
		EQUITIES								
BUY I SELL	ABS	ABS-CBN CORPORATION	9.49	47.2000	50.8316	100	100	4,673.29	-409.87	-8.06%
BUY I SELL	FNI	GLOBAL FERRONICKEL HOLDINGS	62.06	0.8800	0.8915	35,000	35,000	30,555.14	-647.36	2.07%
BUY I SELL	MEG	MEGAWORLD CORPORATION	9.53	4.7400	3.8230	1,000	1,000	4,693.19	870.19	22.76%
BUY I SELL	MER	MANILA ELECTRIC COMPANY	18.92	313.0000	311.7170	30	30	9,315.35	-36.16	-0.39%
						TOTAL EQUITIES		49,236.97		
						TOTAL EQUITIES GAIN/LOSS			-223.20	
						TOTAL PORTFOLIO TRADE VALUE:		49,236.97		
						DAY CHANGE:	0.00%	0.00		
						PORTFOLIO GAIN/LOSS:	-0.48%	-223.20		

Your Total Account Equity Value is 49,885.99

Figure 4

If you will see my portfolio on July 6, 2016, it is only Php. 49,885.99; actually, for more than a year, I haven't funded my investment and just keep one company worth Php. 4,000+ market value when I decided to sell and switch to other company without analyzing potential growth. Why did this happen? Yes, because during those days, I hadn't renewed my TrulyRichClub subscription, that is why I didn't know which company to buy when I decided to invest again in the Stock Market.

Don't Procrastinate...We can do it!

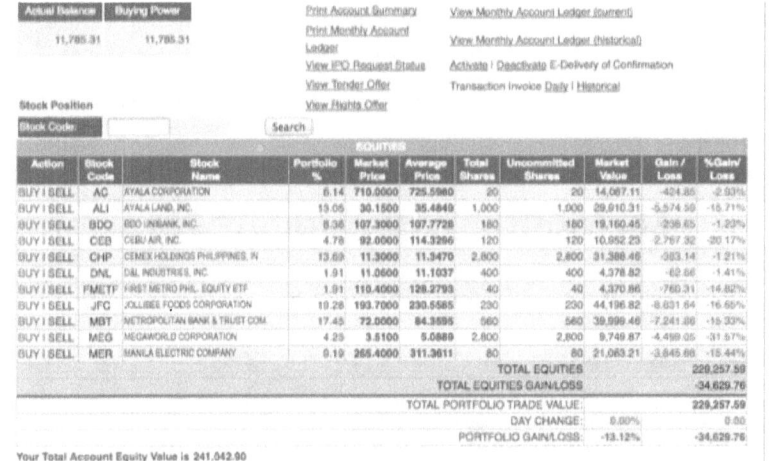

Stock Position

Stock Code:		Search

EQUITIES

Action	Stock Code	Stock Name	Portfolio %	Market Price	Average Price	Total Shares	Uncommitted Shares	Market Value	Gain / Loss	%Gain/ Loss
BUY I SELL	AC	AYALA CORPORATION	6.14	710.0000	725.5980	20	20	14,067.11	-424.85	-2.93%
BUY I SELL	ALI	AYALA LAND, INC.	13.05	30.1500	35.4849	1,000	1,000	29,910.31	-5,574.50	-15.71%
BUY I SELL	BDO	BDO UNIBANK, INC.	8.36	107.3000	107.7728	180	180	19,160.31	-236.65	-1.23%
BUY I SELL	CEB	CEBU AIR, INC.	4.78	92.0000	114.3296	120	120	10,952.23	-2,767.32	-20.17%
BUY I SELL	CHP	CEMEX HOLDINGS PHILIPPINES, IN	13.69	11.3000	11.3470	2,800	2,800	31,386.46	-383.14	-1.21%
BUY I SELL	DNL	D&L INDUSTRIES, INC.	1.91	11.0600	11.1037	400	400	4,378.82	-62.56	-1.41%
BUY I SELL	FMETF	FIRST METRO PHIL. EQUITY ETF	1.91	110.4000	128.2793	40	40	4,370.86	-760.31	-14.82%
BUY I SELL	JFC	JOLLIBEE FOODS CORPORATION	19.28	193.7000	230.5585	230	230	44,196.82	-8,631.64	-16.55%
BUY I SELL	MBT	METROPOLITAN BANK & TRUST COM	17.45	72.0000	84.3595	560	560	39,999.46	-7,241.86	-15.33%
BUY I SELL	MEG	MEGAWORLD CORPORATION	4.25	3.5100	5.0889	2,800	2,800	9,749.87	-4,459.05	-31.57%
BUY I SELL	MER	MANILA ELECTRIC COMPANY	9.19	265.4000	311.3611	80	80	21,063.21	-3,845.66	-15.44%

TOTAL EQUITIES		229,257.59
TOTAL EQUITIES GAIN/LOSS		-34,629.76
TOTAL PORTFOLIO TRADE VALUE:		229,257.59
DAY CHANGE:	0.00%	0.00
PORTFOLIO GAIN/LOSS:	-13.12%	-34,629.76

Your Total Account Equity Value is 241,042.90

Figure 5

So, what did I do? I paid off my annual TrulyRichClub so that I will regain my access to TrulyRichClub members ONLY web page in order to be updated in SAM's table so that I can start buying companies again. If you will see in figure 5, in just 5 months on December 28, 2016, I able to invest around Php. 241,042.90 because of the pressure I put on myself. The plan was to have 1 million investments in the Stock Market on or before my 40th birthday this year 2017. If you will notice, my portfolio losses went up more than Php. 34,000.00 but I still keep funding my COL account and continue buying stocks based on brother Bo Sanchez SAM's table. Why? Yes, once again, because we TrulyRichClub members are truly long-term investors. We are not supposed to be afraid when the stocks market goes down or sideways, in fact, this is an opportunity to buy some more shares as long as following SAM's table. Just disregards my JFC because that is already one of my favorite company for my youngest daughter Maryam.

Six Months Later Update N<u>o</u>.5

January 2, 2017

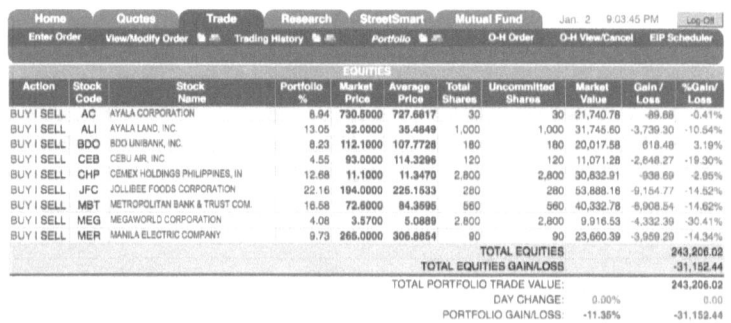

Action	Stock Code	Stock Name	Portfolio %	Market Price	Average Price	Total Shares	Uncommitted Shares	Market Value	Gain / Loss	%Gain/ Loss
BUY I SELL	AC	AYALA CORPORATION	8.94	730.5000	727.6817	30	30	21,740.78	-89.88	-0.41%
BUY I SELL	ALI	AYALA LAND, INC.	13.05	32.0000	35.4849	1,000	1,000	31,745.60	-3,739.30	-10.64%
BUY I SELL	BDO	BDO UNIBANK, INC.	8.23	112.1000	107.7728	180	180	20,017.58	818.48	3.19%
BUY I SELL	CEB	CEBU AIR, INC.	4.55	93.0000	114.3296	120	120	11,071.28	-2,848.27	-19.30%
BUY I SELL	CHP	CEMEX HOLDINGS PHILIPPINES, IN	12.68	11.1000	11.3470	2,800	2,800	30,832.91	-938.69	-2.95%
BUY I SELL	JFC	JOLLIBEE FOODS CORPORATION	22.16	194.0000	225.1533	280	280	53,888.18	-9,154.77	-14.52%
BUY I SELL	MBT	METROPOLITAN BANK & TRUST COM.	16.58	72.6000	84.3695	560	560	40,332.78	-6,908.54	-14.62%
BUY I SELL	MEG	MEGAWORLD CORPORATION	4.08	3.5700	5.0889	2,800	2,800	9,916.53	-4,332.39	-30.41%
BUY I SELL	MER	MANILA ELECTRIC COMPANY	9.73	266.0000	306.8854	90	90	23,660.39	-3,959.29	-14.34%
							TOTAL EQUITIES			243,206.02
							TOTAL EQUITIES GAIN/LOSS			-31,152.44
							TOTAL PORTFOLIO TRADE VALUE:			243,206.02
							DAY CHANGE:	0.00%		0.00
							PORTFOLIO GAIN/LOSS:	-11.36%		-31,152.44

Your Total Account Equity Value is 243,805.02

Figure 6

January 5, 2017

| Home | Quotes | Trade | Research | StreetSmart | Mutual Fund | Jan. 5 | 3:39:27 AM | Log-Off |
| Enter Order | View/Modify Order | Trading History | | Portfolio | | O-H Order | O-H View/Cancel | EIP Scheduler |

Action	Stock Code	Stock Name	Portfolio %	Market Price	Average Price	Total Shares	Uncommitted Shares	Market Value	Gain / Loss	%Gain/ Loss
BUY I SELL	AC	AYALA CORPORATION	8.98	760.0000	727.6817	30	30	22,618.74	788.29	3.61%
BUY I SELL	ALI	AYALA LAND, INC.	13.11	33.3000	35.4849	1,000	1,000	33,035.27	-2,449.64	-6.90%
BUY I SELL	BDO	BDO UNIBANK, INC.	8.15	114.9000	107.7726	180	180	20,517.58	1,118.47	5.77%
BUY I SELL	CEB	CEBU AIR, INC.	4.40	93.0000	114.3296	120	120	11,071.28	-2,648.27	-19.30%
BUY I SELL	CHP	CEMEX HOLDINGS PHILIPPINES, IN	12.48	11.3000	11.3470	2,800	2,800	31,386.46	-383.14	-1.21%
BUY I SELL	JFC	JOLLIBEE FOODS CORPORATION	22.72	206.0000	225.1533	280	280	57,221.44	-5,821.48	-9.23%
BUY I SELL	MBT	METROPOLITAN BANK & TRUST COM.	16.32	74.0000	84.3595	560	560	41,110.55	-6,130.77	-12.98%
BUY I SELL	MEG	MEGAWORLD CORPORATION	4.05	3.6700	5.0889	2,800	2,800	10,194.31	-4,054.61	-28.46%
BUY I SELL	MER	MANILA ELECTRIC COMPANY	9.82	277.0000	306.6854	90	90	24,731.81	-2,887.88	-10.46%
							TOTAL EQUITIES		251,889.43	
							TOTAL EQUITIES GAIN/LOSS		-22,469.03	
						TOTAL PORTFOLIO TRADE VALUE:		251,889.43		
						DAY CHANGE:		0.00%	0.00	
						PORTFOLIO GAIN/LOSS:		-8.19%	-22,469.03	

Your Total Account Equity Value is 252,514.35

Figure 7

If you will notice above the power of investing in the stock market, by just following the very simple steps and system of TrulyRichClub, my portfolios regained Php. 8709.00 losses in just 3-days. Wasn't that an incredible increase?

		My Stocks		
Stock	Shares	Last	Change	%Change
AC	30	760.00	33.00	4.54%
ALI	1,000	33.30	1.30	4.06%
BDO	180	114.90	2.90	2.59%
CEB	120	93.00	3.00	3.33%
CHP	2,800	11.30	0.24	2.17%
JFC	280	206.00	6.00	3.00%
MBT	560	74.00	1.20	1.65%
MEG	2,800	3.67	0.13	3.67%
MER	90	277.00	7.00	2.59%

Figure 8

Imagine if you have invested millions in the stock market in such scenario. How many thousand pesos if not million can your moneymaking machine be able to produce in just few days? Many newbies struggling to understand what was or is going on during the ups and downs and sideways of in the stocks market, why they are losing lots of money in just few minutes. Why? Yes because they weren't following a good system. They want to do it by themselves without understanding at least the basic technical analysis or at least seeking an advice from those experts. To us, being TrulyRichClub members, we don't need to do that anymore, we trusted brother Bo, his recourses, and the system. Brother Bo always notifies us what we need to do during ups and downs or sideways of the stock market through the SAM's table, his stock updates, speculation, news, and most of all the motivational letters, videos, and emails that he provided to all TrulyRichClub members.

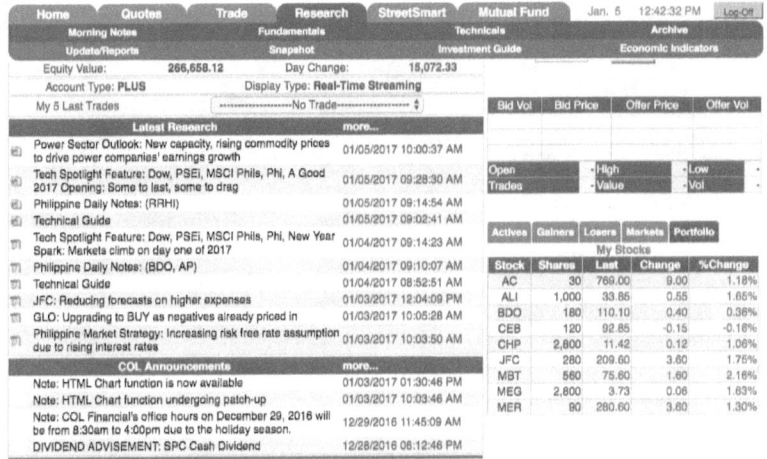

Figure 9

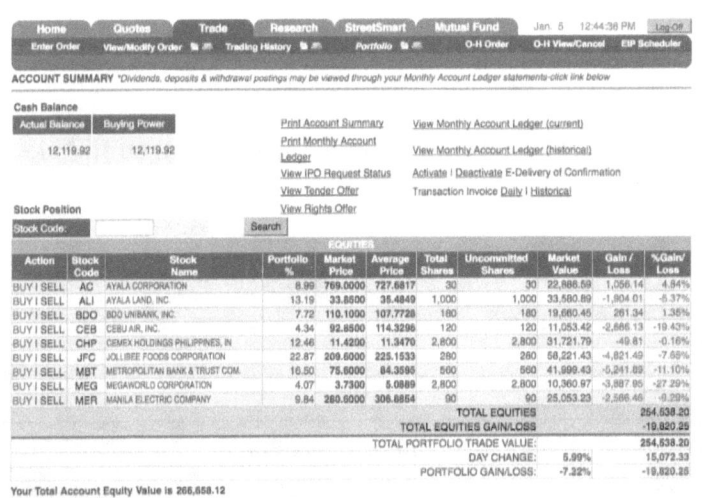

Figure 10

January 5, 2017 @ 2:38PM

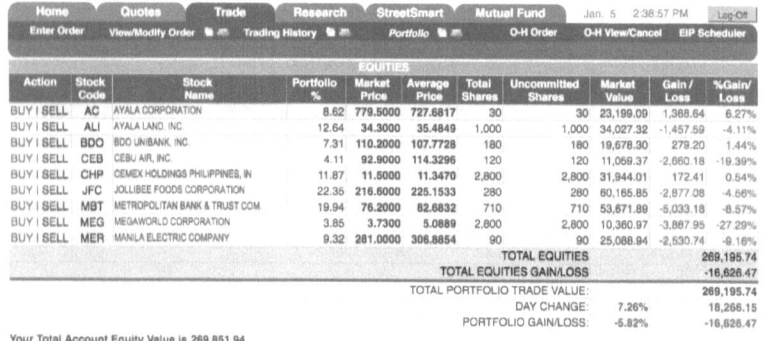

Figure 11

Update No.6

January 6, 2017 @ 11:12AM

Just for 3 days my loss for about 40K decreased to 15K+

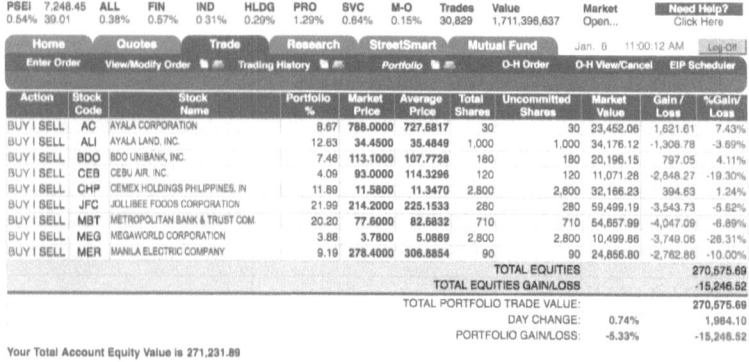

Figure 12

Don't Procrastinate...We can do it!

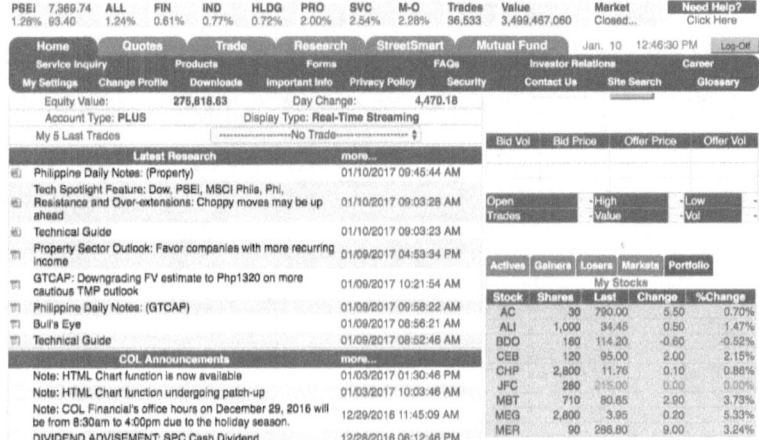

Figure 13

Action	Stock Code	Stock Name	Portfolio %	Market Price	Average Price	Total Shares	Uncommitted Shares	Market Value	Gain / Loss	%Gain/ Loss
BUY I SELL	AC	AYALA CORPORATION	8.54	790.0000	727.6817	30	30	23,511.59	1,681.13	7.70%
BUY I SELL	ALI	AYALA LAND, INC.	12.42	34.4500	35.4849	1,000	1,000	34,176.12	-1,308.78	-3.69%
BUY I SELL	BDO	BDO UNIBANK, INC.	7.41	114.2000	107.7728	180	180	20,392.58	993.48	5.12%
BUY I SELL	CEB	CEBU AIR, INC.	4.11	95.0000	114.3296	120	120	11,309.37	-2,410.18	-17.57%
BUY I SELL	CHP	CEMEX HOLDINGS PHILIPPINES, IN	11.87	11.7600	11.3470	2,800	2,800	32,666.22	894.62	2.82%
BUY I SELL	JFC	JOLLIBEE FOODS CORPORATION	21.70	215.0000	225.1533	280	280	59,721.41	-3,321.51	-5.27%
BUY I SELL	MBT	METROPOLITAN BANK & TRUST COM.	20.64	80.6500	82.6832	710	710	56,806.27	-1,898.80	-3.23%
BUY I SELL	MEG	MEGAWORLD CORPORATION	3.99	3.9500	5.0889	2,800	2,800	10,972.07	-3,276.85	-23.00%
BUY I SELL	MER	MANILA ELECTRIC COMPANY	9.31	286.8000	306.8854	90	90	25,806.79	-2,012.89	-7.29%

TOTAL EQUITIES: 275,162.43
TOTAL EQUITIES GAIN/LOSS: -10,659.76
TOTAL PORTFOLIO TRADE VALUE: 275,162.43
DAY CHANGE: 1.65% 4,470.18
PORTFOLIO GAIN/LOSS: -3.73% -10,659.76

Your Total Account Equity Value is 275,818.63

Figure 14

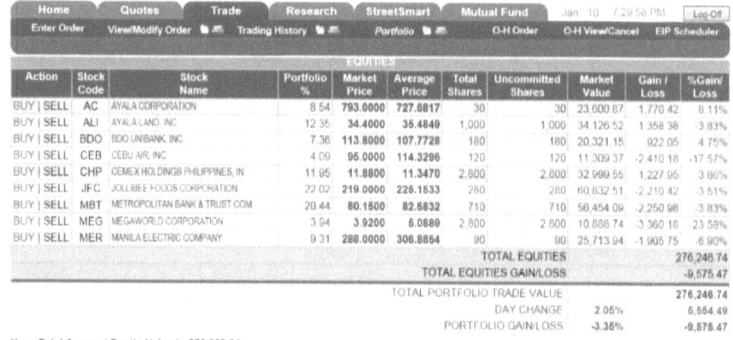

Action	Stock Code	Stock Name	Portfolio %	Market Price	Average Price	Total Shares	Uncommitted Shares	Market Value	Gain / Loss	%Gain/ Loss
BUY | SELL	AC	AYALA CORPORATION	8.54	793.0000	727.6817	30	30	23,600.87	1,770.42	8.11%
BUY | SELL	ALI	AYALA LAND, INC	12.35	34.4000	36.4849	1,000	1,000	34,126.52	-1,358.38	-3.83%
BUY | SELL	BDO	BDO UNIBANK, INC	7.36	113.8000	107.7728	180	180	20,321.15	922.05	4.75%
BUY | SELL	CEB	CEBU AIR, INC	4.09	96.0000	114.3296	120	120	11,309.37	-2,410.18	-17.57%
BUY | SELL	CHP	CEMEX HOLDINGS PHILIPPINES, IN	11.95	11.8800	11.3470	2,800	2,800	32,999.55	1,227.95	3.86%
BUY | SELL	JFC	JOLLIBEE FOODS CORPORATION	22.02	219.0000	226.1633	280	280	60,832.51	-2,210.42	-3.51%
BUY | SELL	MBT	METROPOLITAN BANK & TRUST COM	20.44	80.1500	82.6832	710	710	56,454.09	-2,250.98	-3.83%
BUY | SELL	MEG	MEGAWORLD CORPORATION	3.94	3.9200	6.0889	2,800	2,800	10,888.74	-3,360.18	-23.58%
BUY | SELL	MER	MANILA ELECTRIC COMPANY	9.31	288.0000	306.8854	90	90	25,713.94	-1,905.75	-6.90%

TOTAL EQUITIES			276,246.74
TOTAL EQUITIES GAIN/LOSS			-9,575.47
TOTAL PORTFOLIO TRADE VALUE			276,246.74
DAY CHANGE	2.05%		5,554.49
PORTFOLIO GAIN/LOSS	-3.38%		-9,575.47

Your Total Account Equity Value is 276,902.94

Figure 15

To those who have already started investing in the Stock Market, they may have better balancing on their portfolio. Right now, I am just starting to balance my portfolios and I will do my best to distribute at least 20% of the total value in every company I have. So far, I think I am on the right track. My mentors always said, we shouldn't put all our eggs in one basket. It means we have to invest in different line of business. Right now, I have two similar line of businesses like the banks BDO and MBT, but I love to buy share from those company.

Who knows? **Update No.7**

January 6, 2017 @ 7:00AM – 1:30PM

I meet a potential new future business partner. JC Technology will be the name of our business, we will be in manufacturing line of business.

Our intension to be future business partner was triggered when two of us shared thoughts and plans about business. For 6 hours, we continued our conversation while he explained the proposed business concept with me, I tried to offer if he is interested to partner with me. Well, to me an opportunity like this is seldom to happen. So, I have to decide quickly or take action right away I order to avoid procrastination. Later on, I'll allocate time on assessing the potential or possibility of the proposed business partnership.

Update No.8

January 18, 2017 @ 11:00PM

I completed this book...

Thanks God...

"NEVER GIVE UP, DON'T STOP LEARNING"

Author Bio

I am Jesus G. Pedines Jr., married to Jingle L. Pedines and currently living in Baguio City, Philippines with our two beautiful daughters Aisha and Maryam. I just turned 39 this year 2016 on 27th of November. I was born in Barat Bambang, Nueva Vizcaya Philippines.

Currently, I am working as a safety professional here in Saudi Arabia while managing our financial future in the Stock Market through the guidance of brother Bo Sanchez for being a TrulyRichClub member.

I completed Bachelors of Science in Electrical Engineering at Manuel L. Quezon University, Manila Philippines in 2001. During my childhood, I believed that I could do anything, especially if someone pushed me to do things, even if I knew they were dangerous. I think my skills and talents during my early age, when I was five to ten years old were unbelievable for an ordinary kid. I still remember how I was a fisherman, a tree climber, a sales kid, a singer, and many other talents such as acting and dancing. Until now, I still love to use some of those talents and skills. Yes! I know you, too, had some of those talents and adventurous experiences during your childhood. Am I right? Well, during my high school and college, I showed the same talents to my classmates, friends, and family. I worked for a living to help my parents. I worked at the university every summer vacation, watering the school's orange plantation at Nueva Vizcaya State Polytechnic College, now the Nueva Vizcaya States University. I sold newspapers on the weekends, and at night, I sold eggs or 'Balot.' During college, I sold fried peanuts to my schoolmates in the university especially in the library to earn some extra allowance for going to school. I worked in a fast-food restaurant as service crew, joined a dance group, composed a song, and joined a rock band. My goal during college was not to fail any subject because I had limited financial resources and my parents and my elder sister could not afford it for me to repeat any subjects. So, I did my best and kept my desire to pass all my subjects. Nevertheless, I did it; I graduated with a Bachelor's of Science in Electrical Engineering in 2001. My leadership skills were developed when I and four other friends founded a youth organization in our village called 'Volunteer Brigade.' Although it wasn't officially registered as a youth organization, it helped us to develop our personality and leadership skills. Our goals and objectives were to provide free services to our community. We helped the community on their clean-and-green programs such as tree plantings along the roads and promoting sports activities to the youth.

My father was a carpenter. He worked abroad for seven years and retired from working abroad when I was fourteen. My father bought secondhand tricycles for public transportation to make a living while mother accepted laundry jobs. Our parents always told us, "Education is the only thing they could give us so that we won't be like them." They helped each other to generate our family's daily basic needs and when I was in college my elder sister extended her support for my tuition fees since she had landed her first job. Their determination in running our family was really my inspiration for being good in school so that I could finish my bachelor's degree like my sister. When I graduated college and got a job, I also helped my younger brother until he graduated. It was pretty amazing, isn't it? Well, I would say that's what we are. I am proud to be Filipino.

Professional Background of the Author

In 2003, the author grabbed the opportunity to work abroad as fire safety officer and began to climb the corporate ladder in 2007, then he got an opportunity to work with the biggest oil company in the world, the Saudi Aramco in Saudi Arabia, as a safety advisor at Shaybah GOSP-4 Expansion Projects.

He is an accredited Occupational Safety and Health Practitioner (OSHP) by BWC-DOLE Philippines, a certified Fall Protection Competent Trainer, and has 13 years' experience in safety profession. training, he has developed a wide range of abilities in performing safety and health inspection skills in oil and gas construction industry.

Disclaimer

The material contained in this book is the author's personal way or creativity on sharing his experience as TrulyRichClub member. Neither the publisher and the author nor any companies mentioned herein make any promise or guarantee. The author and/or any financial adviser and brokerage company recommended in this book shall not be liable for any losses or costs of any type arising out of or in any way connected with your use of this book. The book's content is only intended to serve as a guidepost for those who are newbie investor. The author disclaims any and all representations, cannot guarantee, and does not promise any specific results from use of the book. Reader should not make any investment decision without consulting his/her personal financial advisor and or appropriate investment companies or brokerage firms.

Write your first plan here...

Date: _____

_____
_____
_____
_____
_____
_____
_____
_____
_____
_____
_____
_____
_____
_____
_____
_____
_____
_____
_____
_____
_____
_____
_____
_____

_____
_____
_____
_____
_____
_____
_____
_____
_____
_____
_____
_____
_____
_____
_____
_____

_____

Your Name and Signature

_____

Date

CONGRATULATION!!

IF YOU USED ALL PROVIDED 'NOTE SPACE' IN THIS BOOK AND
HAVE ANSWERED ALL EXERCISES, INDEED, YOU HAVE A CHANCE
TO TURN THOSE IDEAS INTO PHYSICAL REALITY.

NOW YOU NEED TO TAKE ACTION...